Debbie Mumm's
QUILTS
from a
Gardener's Journal

D0118451

Enjoy!

From the vibrant amaryllis of January and the peaceful birdbath of May, to the harvest of pears in September and the delight of roses in December ~ Follow the year with this garden full of quilting inspiration!

DEBBIE MUMM

Lupine Leaf

Dear Friends,

Have you heard the term "serendipity?" Where something wonderful happens and everything just seems to come together as if it's meant to be? That's how I feel about Quilts from a Gardener's Journal. From the very beginning, everything for this book just seemed to fall into place. And the result is gorgeous! I couldn't be happier, or more proud, than I am with this beautiful book.

Inspired by my Gardener's Journal artwork, we knew immediately that this book would be a journal in format and that we would trace the passing of the months with quilting projects and garden musings. Deciding on the projects for each month was an easy task and the quilts and craft projects perfectly capture the joys, beauty, and contentment gardening brings into our lives.

Our month-to-month format lent itself perfectly to adding a special "block of the month" quilt as part of this book. Individual blocks from the wonderful Garden Glories Quilt are featured each month so even with our busy days, we can find time to make a flower-filled quilt of lasting beauty.

Delightful Daisies

Sweet Pink Impatie

Vibrant Geranium

Photography for this book was a lot of fun as we wanted a very natural look for all the photos. We traveled from a lavender field, to a stone house, to a beautiful shade garden for our photography settings. The results are spectacular natural settings for our garden-inspired projects.

Cosmos

I hope that you will take your time to relax and enjoy the beautiful photography and journal entries in this book. It is my hope that you will use this book, both for project inspiration as well as to make your own journal entries on the quilting and gardening joys that brighten your life.

Enjoy!

Debbie Mumm

Garden Glories
Block of the Month Quilt

Table of Contents

COLOR PENCIL red

Read in the bulb catalog that the amaryllis was named after a shepherdess in Greek mythology. The word actually means "sparkling." I sure agree!

Amaryllis

Amaryllis
~ So easy to grow!
~ A pot, a saucer, and planting soil
~ Water and place in a warm room

Morning snow

Evergreen shrub

January 5
A glorious amaryllis brings color and life to my living room during this darkest time of the year. Just a few weeks ago, I planted the humble brown bulb and watched joyfully as it grew before my eyes. This week it unfurled a magnificent trumpet-shaped bloom ... its delicious candy-red color and perfect petals are a treat for winter-weary eyes.

pin oak

chestnut

Holly

Welcoming Berry Bush

Bayberry

WINTER AMARYLLIS

38" x 54" WALL QUILT

This amazing amaryllis can bring joy and color to your winter-weary home! Accented with embroidery and beads, the trumpeting flower is an easy appliqué project. A pieced ribbon border makes this wall quilt a joy to behold.

FABRIC REQUIREMENTS AND CUTTING INSTRUCTIONS

Read all instructions before beginning and use 1/4"-wide seam allowances throughout. Read Cutting the Strips and Pieces on page 108 prior to cutting fabrics.

Winter Amaryllis Wall Quilt 38" x 54"	FIRST CUT		SECOND CUT	
	Number of Strips or Pieces	Dimensions	Number of Pieces	Dimensions
Fabric A Background 1 1/4 yards* (directional) or 3/4 yard (non-directional)	1	40 1/2" x 42"	1	40 1/2" x 24 1/2"
Fabric B Border Background 2/3 yard	7	3" x 42"	20 40	3" x 5 1/2" 3" squares
Fabric C Medium Ribbon 5/8 yard	2 2	6 1/2" x 42" 3" x 42"	10 20	6 1/2" x 5 1/2" 3" squares
Fabric D Dark Ribbon 1/3 yard	3	3" x 42"	16 8	3" x 5 1/2" 3" squares
BORDERS				
First Border 1/6 yard	4	1" x 42"	2 2	1" x 24 1/2" 1" x 41 1/2"
Second Border 1/4 yard	4	1 1/2" x 42"		
Binding 1/2 yard	5	2 3/4" x 42"		

Appliqué Flowers - assorted scraps to total 1/2 yard
Appliqué Leaves - assorted scraps to total 1/3 yard
Appliqué Stem - 1/8 yard
Beads - 5
Embroidery Floss
Lightweight Fusible Web - 2 yards
Backing - 1 3/4 yard (must be 44" or wider)
Batting - 44" x 60"
*For directional fabric the measurement listed first runs parallel to selvage (strip width).

Winter Peppers

MAKING THE QUILT

This quilt features a large floral appliqué and a pieced border. Whenever possible, use the Assembly Line Method on page 108. Press in direction of arrows. Refer to Accurate Seam Allowance on page 108 prior to making pieced border.

APPLIQUÉING THE CENTER PANEL

The instructions given are for the Quick-Fuse Appliqué method. If you prefer traditional hand appliqué, be sure to reverse all appliqué templates and add 1/4" seam allowances when cutting appliqué pieces. Refer to Hand Appliqué directions on page 109.

1. Refer to Quick-Fuse Appliqué directions on page 109. Trace appliqué templates on page 9 for eighteen amaryllis petals and six leaves. Trace 1 1/2" x 30" piece for stem. Use assorted scraps to fuse and cut eighteen amaryllis petals, six leaves, and stem.

2. Refer to quilt layout on page 7 and photo on page 5. Position and fuse stem to Fabric A piece. Refer to Appliqué Pressing Sheet on page 109 and arrange amaryllis petals in different directions with petals overlapping and fuse together. Position and fuse amaryllis petal unit on top of stem and leaves on stem, curving them as shown. Finish appliqué edges with machine satin stitch or decorative stitching as desired.

ASSEMBLY

1. Sew 1" x 24½" First Border strips to top and bottom of quilt. Press toward border.

2. Sew 1" x 41½" First Border strips to sides of quilt. Press toward border.

3. Sew 1½" x 42" Second Border strips end to end to make one continuous 1½"-wide strip. Measure quilt through center from side to side. Cut two 1½"-wide Second Border strips to that measurement. Sew to top and bottom of quilt.

4. Measure quilt through center from top to bottom including borders just added. Cut two 1½"-wide Second Border strips to that measurement. Sew to sides of quilt. Press.

5. Refer to Quick Corner Triangles on page 108. Sew 3" Fabric C square to 3" Fabric D square as shown. Press. Make four.

C = 3 x 3
D = 3 x 3
Make 4

6. Sew 3" Fabric B square to unit from step 5 as shown. Press. Make four.

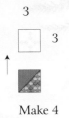

Make 4

7. Making quick corner triangle units, sew 3" Fabric C square and 3" Fabric B square to 3" x 5½" Fabric D piece as shown. Press. Make sixteen.

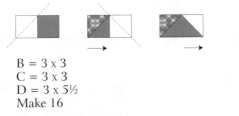

B = 3 x 3
C = 3 x 3
D = 3 x 5½
Make 16

8. Sew unit from step 7 to 3" x 5½" Fabric B piece as shown. Press. Make fourteen.

Make 14

9. Making quick corner triangle units, sew 3" Fabric D square to 3" x 5½" Fabric B piece as shown. Press. Make four, two of each variation.

D = 3 x 3
B = 3 x 5½

D = 3 x 3
B = 3 x 5½
Make 4
(2 of each variation)

Winter Amaryllis Wall Quilt
Finished Size: 38" x 54"; Photo: page 5

10. Sew one unit from step 7 to first unit from step 9. Press. Make two.

Make 2

11. Making quick corner triangle units, sew two 3" Fabric B squares to 6$\frac{1}{2}$" x 5$\frac{1}{2}$" Fabric C piece as shown. Press. Make ten.

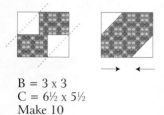

B = 3 x 3
C = 6$\frac{1}{2}$ x 5$\frac{1}{2}$
Make 10

12. Arrange and sew two units from step 6, two units from step 11, and two units from step 8 as shown. Press. Make two. Border unit measures 5$\frac{1}{2}$" x 27$\frac{1}{2}$".

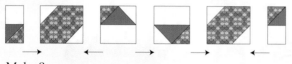

Make 2

13. Arrange and sew one unit from step 9, five units from step 8, three units from step 11, one unit from step 10, and 3" x 5$\frac{1}{2}$" Fabric B piece as shown. Press. Make two. Border unit measures 5$\frac{1}{2}$" x 53$\frac{1}{2}$".

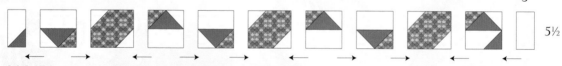

Make 2

14. Refer to quilt layout on page 7 and photo on page 5. Sew border units from step 12 to top and bottom of quilt. Press.

15. Sew border units from step 13 to sides of quilt. Press.

LAYERING AND BINDING

1. Arrange and baste backing, batting, and top together, referring to Layering the Quilt on page 110.

2. Hand or machine quilt as desired.

3. Sew the 2$\frac{3}{4}$" x 42" binding strips end to end to make one continuous 2$\frac{3}{4}$"-wide strip. Refer to Binding the Quilt on page 111, and bind quilt to finish.

4. Refer to quilt layout on page 7, photo on page 5, and Embroidery Stitches on page 108 to add stem stitch embroidery and beads to amaryllis flower.

3

5$\frac{1}{2}$

A Journal Record for Your Quilts

Just like personal and garden journals, a journal record on the back of each quilt will provide valuable information for future generations. To do this, place a label on the back of each quilt you make with the following information.

Name: Naming your quilt will give some insight to your feelings while making the quilt or the type of blocks used in the quilt.

Constructed by: Name of the person or persons who pieced or appliquéd the quilt. Also include the city, state, or country where it was made.

Quilted by: Name of person or persons who hand or machine quilted the quilt.

Date: The month and year the quilt was finished.

Owner's Name: If different than maker.

Occasion: Personal reason for making the quilt. For example: someone's wedding, birthday, graduation, a class taught by a particular teacher, etc.

You may also wish to make a personal quilt journal for yourself by arranging a photo of each finished quilt, samples of fabrics used, and all the information above on pages to place in a binder.

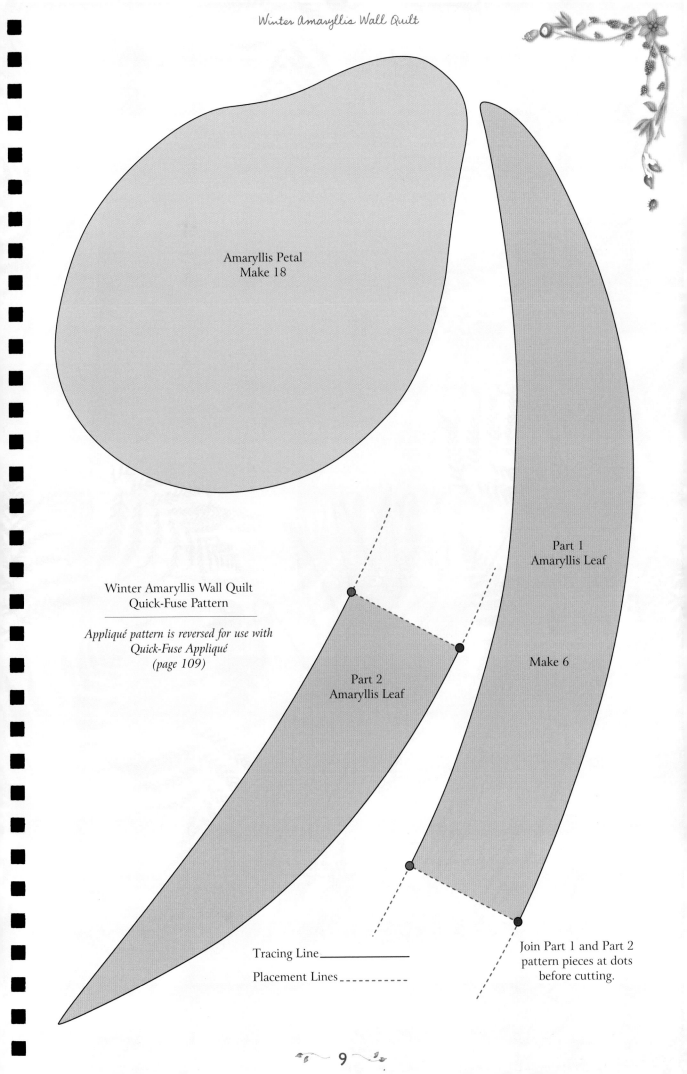

Amaryllis Petal
Make 18

Winter Amaryllis Wall Quilt
Quick-Fuse Pattern

*Appliqué pattern is reversed for use with
Quick-Fuse Appliqué
(page 109)*

Part 1
Amaryllis Leaf

Make 6

Part 2
Amaryllis Leaf

Tracing Line _____

Placement Lines _ _ _ _ _ _ _

Join Part 1 and Part 2
pattern pieces at dots
before cutting.

Debbie Mumm's®
Garden Glories
BLOCK
of the
MONTH

Garden Glories Quilt General Fabric Requirements Finished Size: 67" x 67"	YARDAGE
Center Panel Background & Cornerstones	7/8 yard
Flower Backgrounds	Three fabrics to total 1 7/8 yards
Flowers	Thirteen fabrics to total 2 3/4 yards
Stems and Leaves	Assorted fabrics to total 5/8 yard
Birdbath Base	1/8 yard
Floral Center Panels and Outside Border	3 2/3 yards *
Panel Accent	1/2 yard
Sashing	7/8 yard
Center/ First Border	5/8 yard
Second Border and Ground	1/3 yard
Binding	5/8 yard

Birdbath Accents - Assorted scraps
Bird & Bug Appliqués - Assorted scraps
Decorative Buttons
Embroidery Floss
Beads
Backing - 4 1/8 yards
Batting - 74" x 74"

* Directional fabric was used; if non-directional fabric is desired, 1 1/2 yards of fabric is needed.

Getting Started

Enjoy the glories of the garden all year long when you make this beautiful quilt. Each month we present a new block for you to make so your quilt will come together step by step, month by month. By December, all the blocks will be completed so that you can enjoy finishing your quilt as the year comes to an end.

The quilt consists of the Birdbath Center Panel, eight flower blocks and four Bug Cornerstones. Finished quilt size is 67" x 67". Read all instructions before beginning and use 1/4" seam allowances throughout. Read Cutting the Strips and Pieces on page 108 prior to cutting fabrics. Whenever possible use the Assembly Line Method on page 108. Press in the direction of arrows. Refer to Accurate Seam Allowance on page 108 prior to sewing.

The fabric chart gives you the total yardage needed to complete this quilt. Refer to the quilt photo and individual block fabric charts to determine flower, stem, leaf, and background colors for each block.

Follow the easy step-by-step instructions for each block.
Incorporate the blocks in a unique border treatment to complete this stunning quilt.

Several blocks are on the bias and it is important to stay-stitch where indicated in the block instructions to prevent the stretching of bias seams.

All dimensional flower center treatments will be added to quilt top after quilting is completed. See pages 106-107.

Nasturtium

Daffodils in Bloom

February 23
"I wandered lonely as a cloud
That floats on high o'er vales and hills,
When all at once I saw a crowd—
A host of golden daffodils
Beside the lake, beneath the trees,
Fluttering and dancing in the breeze..."
        William Wordsworth

Flower spray

Daffodils
One of the best loved garden plants
Beautiful, versatile, durable
First large flowers of spring

Pretty in Pink

Just a few warm days and already the daffodils are peeking from the earth!
I can hardly wait until that golden crowd begins their gleeful dance beneath my trees!

Dancing daffodils

There's nothing more rewarding than seeing early sprouts in my garden!

"...and then my heart with pleasure fills,
And dances with the daffodils."
        W.W.

EARLY DAFFODILS

28 1/2" × 51" WALL QUILT

Daffodils emerge from their bulbs to dance in the breeze on this stunning wall quilt. The unusual shape draws the eye while sweet colors soothe the soul. Daffodils and bulbs are easily pieced and leaves are appliquéd.

FABRIC REQUIREMENTS AND CUTTING INSTRUCTIONS

Read all instructions before beginning and use 1/4"-wide seam allowances throughout. Read Cutting the Strips and Pieces on page 108 prior to cutting fabrics.

Early Daffodils Wall Quilt 28 1/2" x 51"	FIRST CUT		SECOND CUT	
	Number of Strips or Pieces	Dimensions	Number of Pieces	Dimensions
DAFFODIL BLOCK				
Fabric A Background 7/8 yard	1	14" x 42"	1	14" x 23"
			1	12 1/4" square
	1	8 1/2" x 42"	1	8 1/2" square
			2	5 1/2" x 2 3/4"
			6	3 1/2" squares
	1	3" x 42"	6	3" squares
			6	2 1/2 squares
	2	1 1/2" x 42"	3	1 1/2" x 5 1/2"
			3	1 1/2" x 4 1/2"
			27	1 1/2" squares
Fabric B Yellow Flower Petals *Assorted scraps to total 1/4 yard*	3	3 1/2" squares		
	9	3 1/2" x 2 1/2"		
	3	2 1/2" x 4 1/2"		
	9	1 1/2" squares		
Fabric C Orange Flower Petals *Assorted scraps to total 1/8 yard*	6	3 1/2" squares		
	3	2 1/2" squares		
Fabric D Bulbs *Scraps*	3	5 1/2" x 6 1/2"		
Fabric E Ground 1/8 yard	1	3 1/2" x 42"	1	3 1/2" x 23"
BORDERS				
First Border 1/6 yard	4	1" x 42"		
Second Border 1/6 yard	4	1" x 42"		
Outside Border 1/3 yard	4	2" x 42"		
Binding 3/8 yard	4	2 3/4" x 42"		

Leaf & Stem Appliqués - Assorted scraps to total 3/8 yard
Batting - 34" x 56"
Backing - 1 5/8 yards
Embroidery Floss
Lightweight Fusible Web - 1 1/6 yards

MAKING THE BLOCKS

You'll be making three Daffodil Blocks. To give our blocks a scrappy look, we used a variety of different yellows for Fabric B and oranges for Fabric C. Blocks measure 8 1/2" unfinished. Whenever possible, use the Assembly Line Method on page 108 and press in direction of arrows.

ASSEMBLY FOR ONE DAFFODIL BLOCK

1. Referring to Quick Corner Triangles on page 108, sew 3 1/2" Fabric A square to 3 1/2" Fabric C square. Press. Make two.

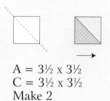

A = 3 1/2 x 3 1/2
C = 3 1/2 x 3 1/2
Make 2

2. Making quick corner triangle units, sew two 1 1/2" Fabric A squares to 3 1/2" x 2 1/2" Fabric B piece as shown. Press. Make two.

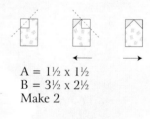

A = 1 1/2 x 1 1/2
B = 3 1/2 x 2 1/2
Make 2

3. Sew units from step 1 to units from step 2 as shown. Press.

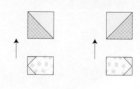

4. Making quick corner triangle units, sew 2½" Fabric A and 2½" Fabric C squares to 2½" x 4½" Fabric B piece as shown. Press.

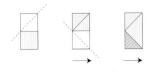

$$A = 2\frac{1}{2} \times 2\frac{1}{2}$$
$$C = 2\frac{1}{2} \times 2\frac{1}{2}$$
$$B = 2\frac{1}{2} \times 4\frac{1}{2}$$

5. Making a quick corner triangle unit, sew two different 1½" Fabric B squares together. Press. Sew unit to 1½" Fabric A square as shown. Press.

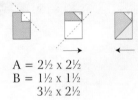

$$B = 1\frac{1}{2} \times 1\frac{1}{2}$$

6. Making quick corner triangle units, sew 1½" Fabric B square and 2½" Fabric A square to 3½" x 2½" Fabric B piece as shown. Press.

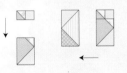

$$A = 2\frac{1}{2} \times 2\frac{1}{2}$$
$$B = 1\frac{1}{2} \times 1\frac{1}{2}$$
$$3\frac{1}{2} \times 2\frac{1}{2}$$

7. Sew unit from step 5 to unit from step 6. Press. Sew to unit from step 4. Press.

8. Sew 1½" x 4½" Fabric A piece to unit from step 7 as shown. Press. Sew 1½" x 5½" Fabric A strip to unit. Press.

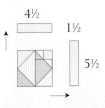

9. Sew first unit from step 3 to unit from step 8 as shown. Press.

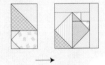

10. Making quick corner triangle units, sew two 1½" Fabric A squares to 3½" Fabric B square as shown. Press.

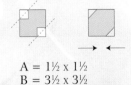

$$A = 1\frac{1}{2} \times 1\frac{1}{2}$$
$$B = 3\frac{1}{2} \times 3\frac{1}{2}$$

11. Sew unit from step 10 to remaining unit from step 3 as shown. Press.

Early Daffodils Wall Quilt
Finished Size: 28½" x 51"; Photo: page 13

12. Sew unit from step 9 to unit from step 11. Press. Block measures 8¹/2" square. Repeat steps 1-12 to make three blocks, one in each color combination.

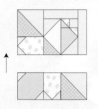

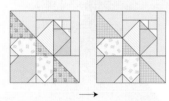

Block measures 8½"
Make 3
(1 of each color combination)

13. Sew three blocks and 8¹/2" Fabric A square together in rows as shown. Press. Sew rows together. Press.

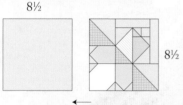

8½

8½

14. Cut 12¹/4" Fabric A square in half once diagonally to make two triangles. Sew one triangle to each side of unit from step 13 as shown. Press toward triangles.

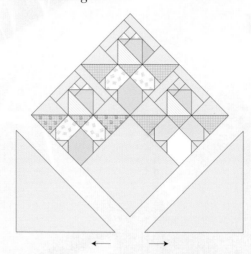

15. Making quick corner triangle units, sew 1¹/2" and 3" Fabric A squares to 5¹/2" x 6¹/2" Fabric D piece as shown. Press. Make three, one of each color combination.

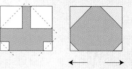

Fabric A = 1½ x 1½
          3 x 3
Fabric D = 5½ x 6½
Make 3
(1 of each color combination)

16. Sew units from step 15 and two 5¹/2" x 2³/4" Fabric A pieces to make row as shown. Press.

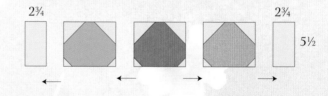

2¾   2¾

5½

17. Sew unit from step 16 to 3¹/2" x 23" Fabric E strip. Press.

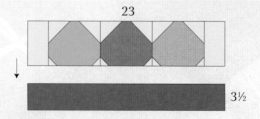

23

3½

18. Referring to quilt layout on page 15 and photo on page 13, sew 14" x 23" Fabric A piece between units from steps 14 and 17. Press.

ADDING THE APPLIQUÉS

The instructions given are for the Quick-Fuse Appliqué method. If you prefer traditional hand appliqué, be sure to reverse all appliqué templates and add 1/4" seam allowances when cutting appliqué pieces. Refer to Hand Appliqué on page 109.

1. Referring to layout on page 15 and Quick-Fuse Appliqué directions on page 109, prepare leaves from templates on page 18 and three 1" x 42" stem appliqués. Arrange leaves and stems on wall hanging. For each outside stem, trim V-shape in blossom end to match daffodil block corner. For center stem, trim an inverted V-shape to match edge of blocks. Trim lower ends of stems even with top of bulbs.

2. Arrange and fuse appliqués in place and finish with machine satin stitch or decorative stitching as desired.

Yellow Petunia Blossoms

BORDERS

1. Refer to quilt layout on page 15 and quilt photo on page 13. Cut 1" x 42" First Border strip in half crosswise. Sew 1"-wide strip to upper right side of quilt. Press seam toward border strip. Trim end of strip even with side of quilt. Sew remaining strip to upper left side of quilt and end of previously sewn border. Press and trim.

2. Sew 1" x 42" First Border strip to bottom edge of quilt. Press seam toward border strip. Trim ends of strip even with quilt. Sew 1" x 42" First Border strips to sides of quilt. Press seams toward border strips and trim even with edges of attached borders.

3. Repeat steps 1 and 2 to sew 1"-wide Second Border and 2"-wide Outside border strips to quilt. Press.

Entries

LAYERING AND FINISHING

1. Layer backing, batting, and top together, referring to Layering the Quilt directions on page 110.

2. Machine or hand quilt as desired.

3. Sew 2³/4" x 42" binding strips end to end to make one continuous 2³/4"-wide strip. Sew 2³/4"-wide binding strip to bottom edge of quilt. Press binding away from quilt. Trim ends of strip even with quilt.

4. Refer to Binding Mitered Corners on page 111 to sew 2³/4"-wide binding strip to sides and top of quilt.

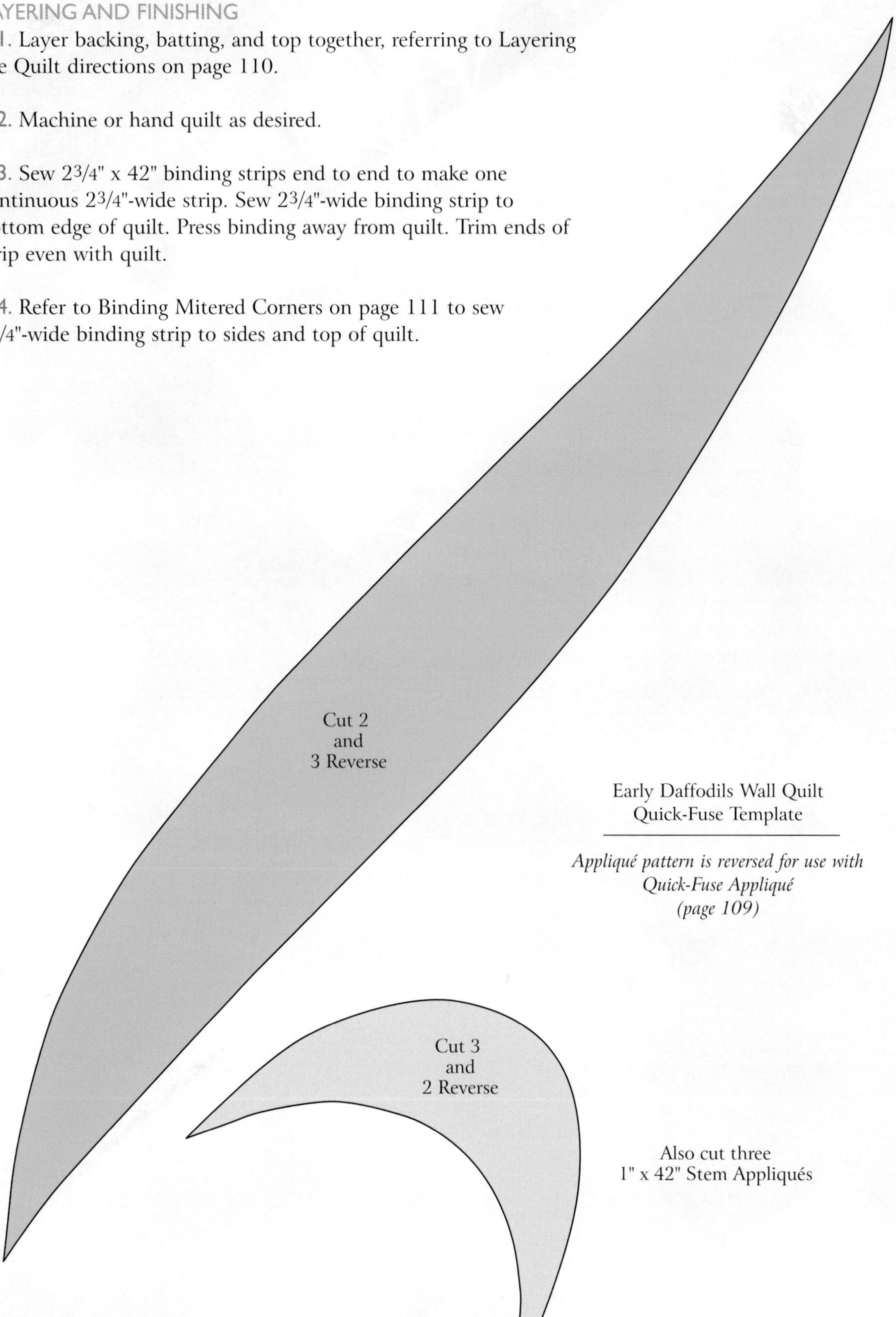

Cut 2
and
3 Reverse

Early Daffodils Wall Quilt
Quick-Fuse Template

*Appliqué pattern is reversed for use with Quick-Fuse Appliqué
(page 109)*

Cut 3
and
2 Reverse

Also cut three
1" x 42" Stem Appliqués

GARDEN GLORIES QUILT

February DAFFODIL

BLOCK OF THE MONTH

February Block of the Month Daffodil (Bottom Right) Garden Glories Quilt photo page 10		
	FIRST CUT	
	Number of Strips or Pieces	Dimensions
▢	1	4¹/₂" square
	2	3¹/₂" squares
Fabric A Background ¹/₄ yard	2	2¹/₂" x 6¹/₂"
	2	2¹/₂" squares
	1	1¹/₂" x 9¹/₂"
	1	1¹/₂" x 8¹/₂"
	1	1¹/₂" x 5¹/₂"
	1	1¹/₂" x 4¹/₂"
	1	1¹/₂" x 3¹/₂"
	1	1¹/₂" x 2¹/₂"
	9	1¹/₂" squares
▦	1	3¹/₂" square
	3	3¹/₂" x 2¹/₂"
Fabric B Daffodil *Assorted yellow scraps*	1	2¹/₂" x 4¹/₂"
	3	1¹/₂" squares
▨	2	3¹/₂" squares
Fabric C Orange Flower Petals *Scrap*	1	2¹/₂" square
▩	1	2¹/₂" square
	1	1¹/₂" x 5¹/₂"
Fabric D Leaves *Assorted scraps*	1	1¹/₂" x 4¹/₂"
	2	1¹/₂" x 3¹/₂"
	2	1¹/₂" squares

Assembly
Refer to Early Daffodils
Wall Quilt steps 1-12
on pages 14-16
to make one
Daffodil Block.

1. Sew 1¹/₂" x 4¹/₂" Fabric D piece to 4¹/₂" Fabric A square. Press. Sew 1¹/₂" x 5¹/₂" Fabric D piece to unit as shown. Press.

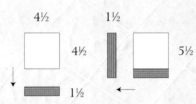

2. Referring to Quick Corner Triangles on page 108, sew 1¹/₂" Fabric A square and 1¹/₂" Fabric D square to 1¹/₂" x 3¹/₂" Fabric D piece as shown. Press. Make two, one of each variation.

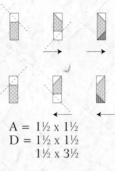

A = 1¹/₂ x 1¹/₂
D = 1¹/₂ x 1¹/₂
1¹/₂ x 3¹/₂

3. Sew one unit from step 2 to 1¹/₂" x 2¹/₂" Fabric A piece as shown. Press. Sew remaining unit from step 2 to 1¹/₂" x 3¹/₂" Fabric A piece as shown. Press.

2¹/₂
1¹/₂

3¹/₂
1¹/₂

4. Sew units from step 3 to sides of unit from step 1 as shown. Press.

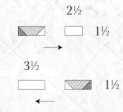

5. Sew 2¹/₂" Fabric D square to 2¹/₂" x 6¹/₂" Fabric A piece as shown. Press. Sew unit from step 4 to 2¹/₂" x 6¹/₂" Fabric A piece as shown. Press. Sew both units together and press.

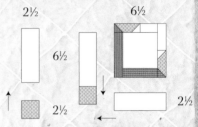

6. Sew unit from step 5 to 1¹/₂" x 8¹/₂" Fabric A piece as shown. Press. Sew 1¹/₂" x 9¹/₂" Fabric A piece to unit. Press. Block measures 9¹/₂" square. Draw a diagonal line on the unit as shown. Stitch 1/8" from each side of the drawn line. Carefully cut unit on drawn line to make two leaf units.

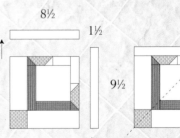

**Block measures
9¹/₂" square**

7. Sew leaf units from step 6 to two sides of the Daffodil block as shown. Press.

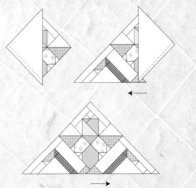

Purple Daisy

Birds of a feather flock together

March 4
A beautiful day with bright
sunshine warming the soil.
The seeds so lovingly planted will
soon be sprouting from the earth ...
fresh new life. A bird seems to have taken
up residence in the old birdhouse on the fence.
With a few more warm days the morning glory
vine will begin to work its way up the fence
to provide our bird guests with their own
garden of gorgeous blooms later
this summer.

Pink Star Morning Glories

Johnny Jump-up

Dainty Dianthus

Morning Glory ~ Delight to grow!
~ Rich colors and velvety texture
~ Abundantly beautiful in summer and fall
~ Perfect for the fence, mailbox, or trellis

Flowers open in
the morning and
close by nightfall

Royal Morning Glories

Love this flower!

From Aunt Edna's Garden

Checklist
☑ Plant climbers
☐ Prune shrubs
☑ Reseed Lawn

MORNING GLORY BIRDHOUSE

24" x 44" DOOR BANNER

Capture that moment when the birds discover their morning glory garden with this beautiful door banner. Dimensional morning glories climb up a fabric fence in this easy piecing project.

FABRIC REQUIREMENTS AND CUTTING INSTRUCTIONS

Read all instructions before beginning and use 1/4"-wide seam allowances throughout. Read Cutting the Strips and Pieces on page 108 prior to cutting fabrics.

Morning Glory Birdhouse Door Banner 24" x 44"	FIRST CUT		SECOND CUT	
	Number of Strips or Pieces	Dimensions	Number of Pieces	Dimensions
Fabric A Background and Nine-patch Corners 1/2 yard	1	8 1/2" x 42"	1	8 1/2" x 8"
			1	8 1/2" x 6 1/2"
			2	7" x 4"
			1	6 1/2" x 2 1/2"
			1	6 1/2" x 2"
			1	5 1/2" x 3"
			1	5 1/2" x 2 1/2"
	1	4 1/2" x 42"	1	4 1/2" x 8"
			1	4 1/2" x 6 1/2"
			1	3 1/2" x 8"
			1	3 1/2" x 6 1/2"
	2	1 1/2" x 42"	1	1 1/2" x 16 1/2"
			2	1 1/2" x 14"
			1	1 1/2" x 8"
Fabric B Fence and Nine-patch Corners 2/3 yard * *For non-directional fabric use 1/3 yard*	1	19 1/2" x 42"	1	19 1/2" x 3"
			2	8" x 2 1/2"
			2	6 1/2" x 2 1/2"
	1	1 1/2" x 42"	1	1 1/2" x 14"
			2	1 1/2" x 8"
Fabric C Birdhouse 1/6 yard	1	4" x 42"	2	4" x 7"
			1	3 1/4" x 12"
Fabric D - Roof 1/6 yard	1	4" x 42"	2	4" x 7"
			1	4" x 6 1/2"
Fabric E Roof Trim 1/8 yard	1	1 1/2" x 42"	2	1 1/2" x 9"
Fabric F Birdhouse Base 3/8 yard* *For non-directional fabric use 1/3 yard*	1	12" x 2 3/4"		"fussy cut" border print
BORDERS				
Accent Border 1/8 yard	3	1" x 42"		
First Border 1/6 yard	3	1 1/2" x 42"		
Second Border 1/6 yard	3	1 1/2" x 42"		
Outside Border 1/6 yard	3	1 1/2" x 42"		

* For directional fabric the measurement listed first runs parallel to selvage (strip width).

Morning Glory Birdhouse Quilt Continued	FIRST CUT	
	Number of Strips or Pieces	Dimensions
Decorative Leaf Edging 1/4 yard each of two fabrics		
Binding 3/8 yard	3	2 3/4" x 42"
	1	1 1/2" x 24"
	1	1" x 24"

Morning Glories - 1/6 yard each color
Leaves and Birds - Assorted scraps
Birdhouse Hole - Scrap
Lightweight Fusible Web - Scrap
Backing - 1 1/4 yards
Batting - 28" x 48"
Silk Ribbon - 2mm and 4mm wide
Perle Cotton or Embroidery Floss

MAKING THE QUILT

You will be using a combination of techniques for this quilt including foundation paper-piecing, quick corner triangles, dimensional and quick-fuse appliqué, and embellishments. Whenever possible, use the Assembly Line Method on page 108. Press in direction of arrows.

ASSEMBLY

1. Make one copy and two copies reversed of paper-piecing pattern on page 26. Cut paper-piecing copies larger than trim line on all sides. Blocks will be cut on trim line after they are completed.

2. Using flat flower-head pins, pin one 7" x 4" Fabric A piece right side up over shape 1 on blank (unprinted) side of paper-piecing pattern. Center it over the area labeled "1." Be sure to cover entire area, extending at least 1/2" on all sides of shape 1. Turn pinned unit to printed side. Fold paper on stitch line between 1 and 2 and trim fabric 1/4" away from fold as shown. Unfold paper.

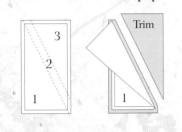

3. With right sides together, position 1 1/2" x 9" Fabric E piece on Fabric A piece, matching edges with piece just trimmed. Pin away from seam line. With printed side up, sew directly on stitch line through paper and both layers of fabric. Use a very short stitch (14-16 stitches per inch). Turn over pattern, fold back section 2 fabric piece, and press. Make sure Fabric E piece completely covers area 2, allowing for 1/4" seam allowance on all sides.

4. Repeat steps 2 and 3 to add 4" x 7" Fabric C piece to Fabric E piece, covering area 3. Press.

5. Using paper pattern for guidance, trim block along trim line to 3 1/2" x 6 1/2".

6. Using reversed pattern, repeat steps 2 through 5 to make second roof unit. Use 4" x 7" Fabric D piece for area 1, 1 1/2" x 9" Fabric E piece for area 2, and 4" x 7" Fabric C piece for area 3. Finger press and trim.

7. Using reversed pattern, repeat steps 2, 3, and 5 to make roof-and-sky unit. Use 7" x 4" Fabric A piece for area 1, and 4" x 7" Fabric D piece for areas 2 and 3 (combined). Sew on line between area 1 and 2. Finger press and trim.

8. Position and sew together 6 1/2" x 2 1/2" and 6 1/2" x 2" Fabric A pieces, 4" x 6 1/2" Fabric D piece, and roof-and-sky paper-pieced units from steps 4, 6, and 7 as shown. Press. Press roof pitch seam open.

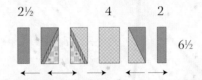

9. Sew 3 1/4" x 12" Fabric C piece to 12" x 2 3/4" Fabric F piece as shown. Press.

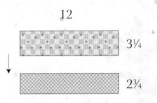

10. Sew unit from step 9 between 5 1/2" x 3" and 5 1/2" x 2 1/2" Fabric A pieces as shown. Press.

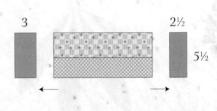

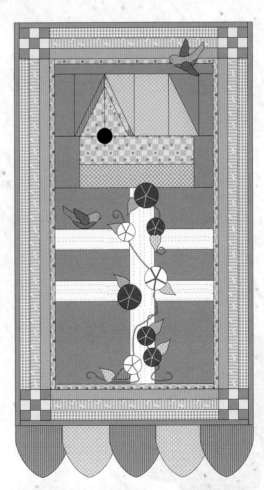

Morning Glory Birdhouse Door Banner
Finished Size: 24" x 44"; Photo: page 21

11. Sew unit from step 8 between 1½" x 16½" Fabric A strip and unit from step 10 as shown. Press. Section measures 16½" x 12½". Remove paper from paper-pieced blocks.

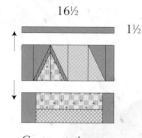

16½

1½

Center section measures 16½" x 12½"

12. Sew together 4½" x 8" Fabric A, 8" x 2½" Fabric B, 3½" x 8" Fabric A, 8" x 2½" Fabric B, and 8½" x 8" Fabric A pieces as shown to make left vertical row. Press. Sew together 4½" x 6½" Fabric A, 6½" x 2½" Fabric B, 3½" x 6½" Fabric A, 6½" x 2½" Fabric B, and 8½" x 6½" Fabric A pieces as shown to make right vertical row. Press.

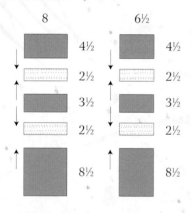

8   6½

4½   4½

2½   2½

3½   3½

2½   2½

8½   8½

13. Sew 19½" x 3" Fabric B strip between units from step 12 as shown. Press.

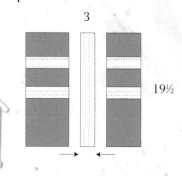

3

19½

14. Sew unit from step 13 to bottom of unit from step 11. Press.

BORDERS

1. Sew three 1" x 42" Accent Border strips together end to end to make one continuous 1"-wide strip. Measure quilt through center from side to side. Cut two 1" Accent Border strips to this measurement. Sew to top and bottom of quilt. Press seams toward borders.

2. Measure quilt through center from top to bottom including borders just added. Cut remaining 1"-wide strip to this measurement. Make two. Sew to sides. Press.

3. Sew 1½" x 14" Fabric B strip between two 1½" x 14" Fabric A strips. Press. From strip set, cut eight 1½"-wide segments. Press.

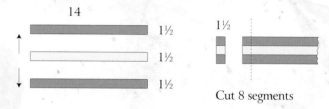

14

1½

1½

1½

1½

Cut 8 segments

4. Sew 1½" x 8" Fabric A strip between two 1½" x 8" Fabric B strips. Press. From strip set, cut four 1½"-wide segments.

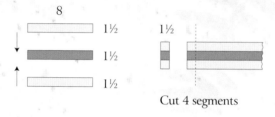

8

1½

1½

1½

1½

Cut 4 segments

5. Sew segment from step 4 between two segments from step 3 as shown. Press. Make four.

Make 4

6. Sew 1½" x 42" First Border, Second Border, and Outside Border strips together lengthwise as shown. Press. Make three sets. Measure quilt through center from side to side. Cut one border strip set into two strips using this measurement. Measure quilt through center from top to bottom. Using remaining border strip sets, cut two pieces to this measurement. Sew short pieced borders to top and bottom of quilt. Press seams toward borders.

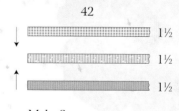

42

1½

1½

1½

Make 3

7. Sew one border strip set from step 6 between two units from step 5. Press seams toward borders. Make two. Sew borders to sides of quilt. Press.

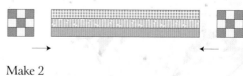

Make 2

APPLIQUÉ

The instructions given are for Quick-Fuse Appliqué. If you prefer traditional hand appliqué, be sure to reverse all appliqué templates and add 1/4"-wide seam allowances when cutting appliqué pieces. Refer to Hand Appliqué directions on page 109.

1. Referring to Quick Fuse Appliqué on page 109, trace appliqué bird pattern from page 26 to paper side of fusible web. Trace patterns for one bird and wing and one bird and two wings reversed. Trace 1 1/2" circle from Circle Templates on page 107 for birdhouse hole.

2. Referring to layout on page 23, position and fuse appliqués in place. Finish with machine satin stitch or decorative stitching as desired.

3. Using Circle Templates on page 107, trace five 2" circles and three 2 1/2" circles on wrong side of Morning Glory fabrics, leaving 1/2" space between each circle. Place traced fabric, right sides together, with a matching piece of fabric and stitch on traced lines. Cut out flowers leaving a 3/16" seam allowance. Clip curves. Slit the back circle and turn right side out. Press.

4. Using Morning Glory Leaf Template on page 26, trace nine leaves on wrong side of leaf fabrics, leaving 1/2" space between each leaf. Place traced fabric, right sides together, with a matching piece of fabric and stitch on traced lines. Cut out leaves leaving a 3/16" seam allowance. Clip curves. Slit back leaf and turn right side out. Press.

LAYERING AND FINISHING

1. With right sides together, position and sew 1" x 24" decorative binding-fabric strip to bottom of quilt. Press. Strip will extend 1/4" beyond edges of quilt.

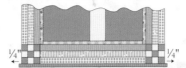

2. Layer backing, batting, and top together, referring to Layering the Quilt directions on page 110.

3. Machine or hand quilt as desired.

4. Using Decorative Leaf Edging Pattern on page 26, cut six leaf shapes from dark leaf fabric and four leaf shapes from light leaf fabric. With right sides together, sew shapes in pairs with a 1/4" seam allowance to make three dark leaves and two light leaves. Clip curves and turn right side out. Press.

Make 5

5. With right sides together, arrange leaves. Overlap and alternate dark and light, starting and ending at edge of decorative-binding strip across bottom of quilt. Baste leaves to quilt. See step 6 diagram.

6. Press under 1/4" along one long edge of 1 1/2" x 24" bottom binding strip. With right sides together, sew unfolded edge of strip to bottom of quilt over leaves as shown. Press strip and leaves down. On back of quilt, press seam allowances and decorative strip up, so leaves will fall gracefully. Fold strip over seam allowances and hand stitch folded edge to back of quilt.

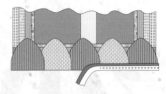

7. Referring to Binding the Quilt on page 111, sew 2 3/4" binding strips to top and sides of quilt; trim to extend 1/4" past bottom of quilt. Fold up this extra 1/4" at end of each binding strip before folding the binding to back of quilt and hand stitching.

8. Referring to photo on page 21 and quilt layout on page 23, use silk ribbon to sew five long stitches from center of each Morning Glory to outer edges to make stripes. Or using two strands of embroidery floss and a stem stitch, sew five accent lines from center of morning glory to outside edges.

9. Referring to photo on page 21 and quilt layout on page 23, sew flowers and leaves to quilt. Using stem stitch and green perle cotton or three strands of embroidery floss, embroider vine on quilt.

Bright as a summer morning

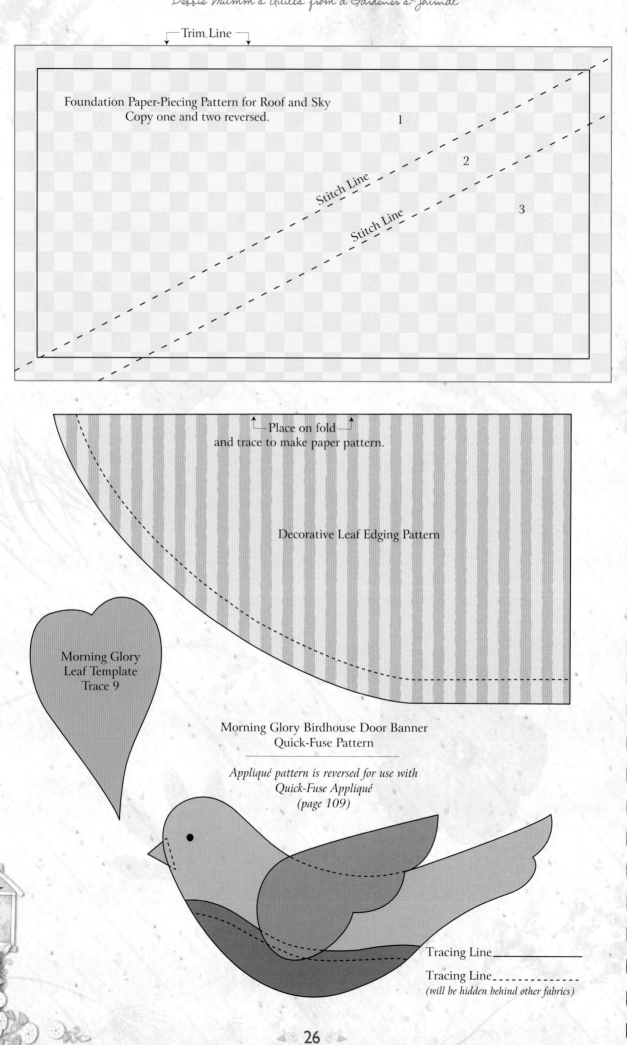

Trim Line

Foundation Paper-Piecing Pattern for Roof and Sky
Copy one and two reversed.

1

2

3

Stitch Line

Stitch Line

Place on fold
and trace to make paper pattern.

Decorative Leaf Edging Pattern

Morning Glory
Leaf Template
Trace 9

Morning Glory Birdhouse Door Banner
Quick-Fuse Pattern

*Appliqué pattern is reversed for use with
Quick-Fuse Appliqué
(page 109)*

Tracing Line _____

Tracing Line _ _ _ _ _ _ _ _ _
(will be hidden behind other fabrics)

March Block of the Month Primrose (Center Bottom) Garden Glories Quilt photo on page 10		
FIRST CUT		
	Number of Strips or Pieces	Dimensions
Fabric A Background 1/8 yard	4	3" squares
	8	2" squares
	8	1 1/2" squares
Fabric B Dark Petals 1/8 yard	2	3 1/2" squares
	4	3" squares
Fabric C Light Petals 1/8 yard	2	3 1/2" squares
	4	3" squares
Fabric D Center 1/8 yard	1	2" × 42"
1" Button		

Assembly

1. Referring to Quick Corner Triangles on page 108, sew 1 1/2" Fabric A square and 2" Fabric A square to 3" Fabric B square as shown. Press. Make four.

A = 1½ x 1½
 2 x 2
B = 3 x 3
Make 4

2. Making quick corner triangle units, sew 1 1/2" Fabric A square and 2" Fabric A square to 3" Fabric C square as shown. Press. Make four.

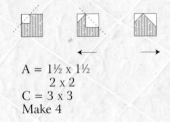

A = 1½ x 1½
 2 x 2
C = 3 x 3
Make 4

3. Make half-square triangles by drawing a diagonal line on wrong side of 3 1/2" Fabric B square. Place one Fabric B square and one 3 1/2" Fabric C square right sides together. Sew a scant 1/4" from both sides of drawn line as shown. Make two. Cut on drawn line. Press. Square to 3". This will make four half-square triangle units.

B = 3½ x 3½
C = 3½ x 3½
Make 2

Square to 3"
Make 4

4. Arrange four 3" Fabric A squares and units from steps 1, 2, and 3, as shown. Sew units into rows. Press. Sew rows together and press. Block measures 10 1/2" square.

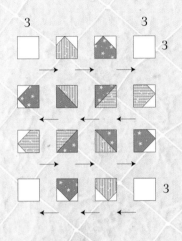

Block measures 10½" square

5. Referring to Making Ruched Flowers on page 106, use 2"-wide Fabric D strip to make 3" flower. After quilting is completed, stitch ruched flower to quilt. Sew button to center of ruched flower.

Entries

_____

_____

_____

_____

Sweet!

Perfect against a building, fence, wall

Planting for the Spring

Old-Fashioned Favorite

Hollyhocks
~ Big and gracious
~ Prized for its kingly height
~ Blooms all summer!

Wild Lupine

April 18
Busy day transplanting
flowers and filling my patio pots.
Thank goodness I have my trusty
wheelbarrow to help me with all the
hauling! Tabby kept me company
this afternoon, lounging in the shade of the
wheelbarrow. Planted the hollyhock seeds the neighbor
gave me next to the garden shed. I can hardly
wait for those stately beauties to bloom!

Daisies and Zinnias

Black-Eyed Susans

IN THE GARDEN
44" x 36" WALL QUILT

The simple joys of gardening can be celebrated all through the year with this sweet garden vignette. A combination of piecing and appliqué make this wall quilt surprisingly easy to construct.

FABRIC REQUIREMENTS AND CUTTING INSTRUCTIONS

Read all instructions before beginning and use 1/4"-wide seam allowances throughout. Read Cutting the Strips and Pieces on page 108 prior to cutting fabrics.

In The Garden Wall Quilt 44" x 36"	FIRST CUT		SECOND CUT	
	Number of Strips or Pieces	Dimensions	Number of Pieces	Dimensions
Fabric A Background *1 yard*	1	16" x 42"	1	16" x 19 1/2"
			1	16" x 6 1/2"
			1	16" x 3"
	1	5" x 42"	1	5" x 20 1/2"
	1	4 1/2" x 42"	1	4 1/2" x 20 1/2"
			1	4 1/2" x 9 1/2"
			1	4 1/2" x 1 1/2"
	1	3 1/2" x 42"	1	3 1/2" x 7"
			1	3 1/2" x 1 1/2"
			1	3" x 5"
			1	3" square
			2	3" x 1"
	1	2 1/2" x 42"	1	2 1/2" x 25 1/2"
			4	1 1/2" squares
			1	1 1/2" x 1"
			1	1" square
Fabric B Cat Face *Scrap*	1	2 1/2" x 3"		
	2	1" squares		
Fabric C Cat Body *1/8 yard*	1	3 1/2" x 6"		
	1	1" x 2"		
	1	1" square		
Fabric D - Basket *Scrap*	2	4" x 4 1/2"		
Fabric E Basket Handle *Scrap*	1	1 1/2" x 7"		
Fabric F Hollyhock Stalks and Leaves *1/8 yard each of three fabrics*	1	1" x 22 1/2" *center stalk*		
	1	1" x 20 1/2" *left stalk*		
	1	1" x 16" *right stalk*		
	1	1" x 3" *right stalk*		
Wheelbarrow *1/4 yard*	1	7 1/2" x 42"	1	7 1/2" x 8 1/2"
			1	7 1/2" x 4 1/2"
Wheelbarrow Trim and Handles *1/8 yard*	2	1 1/2" x 42"	1	1 1/2" x 25"
			3	1 1/2" x 7 1/2"
Fabric G - Grass and Black-Eyed Susan Leaves and Stems *1/8 yard*	1	2 1/2" x 34 1/2"		

In The Garden Wall Quilt, Continued	FIRST CUT	
	Number of Strips or Pieces	Dimensions
BORDERS		
First Border *1/6 yard*	4	1" x 42"
Second Border *1/4 yard*	4	1 1/2" x 42"
Outside Border *1/2 yard*	4	3 1/2" x 42"
Binding *3/8 yard*	4	2 3/4" x 42"

Wheelbarrow Wheel - 1/4 yard
Hollyhocks - 1/6 yard each of five assorted reds
Black-Eyed Susans and Centers, Soil, Plants, and Garden Tools - Assorted scraps
Lightweight Fusible Web - 1 yard
Backing - 1 1/3 yards
Batting - 48" x 40"
3/4" Button

MAKING THE UNITS

You will piece three sections for the background, then use a variety of methods to add the key features to the quilt– quick-fuse, machine, and dimensional appliqué. Press in direction of arrows.

ASSEMBLY

1. Referring to Quick Corner Triangles on page 108, sew two 1" Fabric B squares to 3" x 1" Fabric A piece. Press.

B = 1 x 1
A = 3 x 1

Aster Bloom

2. Making quick corner triangles, sew 1" Fabric A and 1" Fabric C squares to 2½" x 3" Fabric B piece as shown. Press.

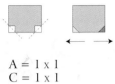

A = 1 x 1
C = 1 x 1
B = 2½ x 3

3. Sew 1½" x 1" Fabric A piece to 1" x 2" Fabric C piece. Press.

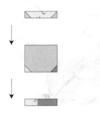

4. Sew unit from step 2 between units from step 1 and step 3 as shown. Press.

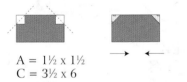

5. Making quick corner triangles, sew two 1½" Fabric A squares to 3½" x 6" Fabric C piece as shown. Press.

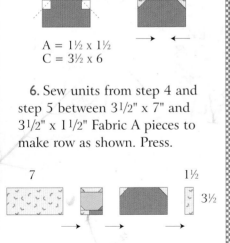

A = 1½ x 1½
C = 3½ x 6

6. Sew units from step 4 and step 5 between 3½" x 7" and 3½" x 1½" Fabric A pieces to make row as shown. Press.

7   1½

3½

7. Sew unit from step 6 to 16" x 19½" Fabric A piece as shown. Press. Sew 1" x 22½" Fabric F strip to side of unit as shown to make center section. Press.

1   16

22½   19½

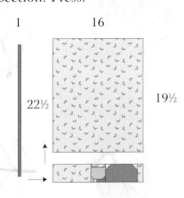

8. Making quick corner triangle units, sew 1½" Fabric A squares to 4" x 4½" Fabric D pieces as shown. Press. Make one of each variation.

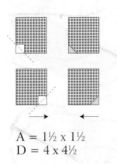

A = 1½ x 1½
D = 4 x 4½

9. Sew 1" x 3" Fabric F piece between 3" Fabric A square and 3" x 1" Fabric A piece as shown. Press.

3 1 1

 3

10. Sew unit from step 9 to first unit from step 8 as shown. Press.

11. Sew 4½" x 1½" Fabric A piece to remaining unit from step 8 as shown. Press.

1½

4½

In The Garden Wall Quilt
Finished Size: 44" x 36"; Photo: page 29

12. Sew unit from step 11 to 3" x 5" Fabric A piece as shown. Press.

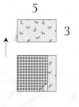

13. Sew 1½" x 7" Fabric E piece between units from step 10 and step 12 to make basket unit. Press.

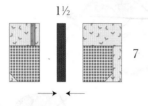

14. Sew 1" x 16" Fabric F strip between 16" x 3" and 16" x 6½" Fabric A pieces. Press. Sew to top of basket unit from step 13 to make right section. Press.

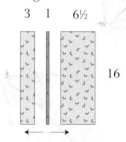

15. Sew 1" x 20½" Fabric F strip between 4½" x 20½" and 5" x 20½" Fabric A pieces. Press. Sew unit to 4½" x 9½" Fabric A piece as shown to make left section. Press.

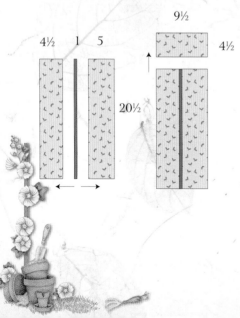

16. Referring to quilt layout on page 31, sew center section from step 7 to right section from step 14. Press. Sew 2½" x 25½" Fabric A strip across top of section. Press seam up. Sew this unit to left section from step 15.

17. Sew 2½" x 34½" Fabric G strip to bottom of quilt. Press.

18. Sew two 1½" x 7½" Wheelbarrow Trim pieces, 7½" x 8½" and 7½" x 4½" Wheelbarrow pieces together as shown. Press.

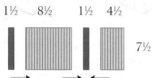

19. Sew 1½" x 25" Wheelbarrow Trim to bottom of unit from step 18 as shown. Refer to quilt layout on page 31 to line up and sew remaining 1½" x 7½" Wheelbarrow Trim piece to 1½" x 25" piece. Place quarter-circle template on page 34 on corner of 4½" x 7" wheelbarrow fabric and trace a rounded corner. Stay stitch on traced line and 3/16" from raw edges of wheelbarrow unit. Trim ¼" from edge of stay stitching on rounded corner. Press stitched edges under.

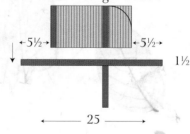

APPLIQUÉ

The instructions given are for Quick-Fuse Appliqué method. If you prefer traditional hand appliqué, be sure to reverse all appliqué templates and add ¼"-wide seam allowances when cutting appliqué pieces. Refer to Hand Appliqué directions on page 109.

1. Referring to Quick-Fuse Appliqué on page 109, prepare eight leaves using Hollyhock Leaf Template on page 34. For hollyhocks use Circle Templates on page 107 to prepare eight 1¾" circles, eight 2" circles, and five 2¼" circles.

2. Referring to quilt layout on page 31, position hollyhock and leaf appliqués along stalks on quilt. Arrange hollyhocks, keeping in mind you will add twelve yo-yos later, so plan a good balance of appliqués and yo-yos.

3. On fusible web, trace the quarter-wheel template on page 34 four times, aligning at dots. Fuse to wheel fabric and cut.

4. Referring to Quick-Fuse Appliqué on page 109, prepare and cut trowel top, two handles, and four plant leaves using templates on page 34. Trace a portion of the wheel template in a semicircle for soil, cutting a few dips in the edges to resemble a pile of soil.

5. Position and pin wheelbarrow on quilt. Referring to quilt layout on page 31, position plant leaves, trowel top, handles, dirt, and wheel on quilt. Place the trim on the tool handles as desired. Fuse appliqués in place. Machine or hand appliqué wheelbarrow to quilt.

6. Referring to quilt layout on page 31, trace, position, and fuse twenty-four Black-Eyed Susan petals, five leaves, four center circles, and two stems to quilt top.

7. Finish quick-fuse appliqué pieces with machine satin stitch or decorative stitching as desired.

BORDERS

1. Sew 1" x 42" First Border strips together end to end to make one continuous 1"-wide strip. Measure quilt through center from side to side. Cut two 1"-wide First Border strips to that measurement. Sew to top and bottom of quilt. Press seam toward first border.

2. Measure quilt through center from top to bottom including borders just added. Cut two 1"-wide First Border strips to that measurement. Sew to sides. Press.

3. Repeat steps 1 and 2 to join, fit, trim, and sew 1½"-wide Second Border strips, and 3½"-wide Outside Border strips to top, bottom, and sides. Press toward each newly added border.

Gardener's Gift

Surprise your favorite gardener with a special gift! What could be nicer than a variety of garden essentials packaged in a charming container made from a hand-painted flowerpot and saucer? These decorative containers are so easy, you'll want to make several!

Materials Needed:

Terra cotta flowerpots and saucers*
Clear sealer
Acrylic paints
Rubber bands in a variety of widths
Removable round dots
Paintbrushes
Spray matte outdoor varnish
Raffia, twine, suede string

When purchasing flowerpots and saucers, select saucers that fit on top of the pots when turned upside down.

Rubber bands and removable dots are the secret to painting these easy pots! Use the rubber bands and dots to mask off areas so the terra cotta color or another color will show through the top layer of paint.

Brush clear sealer on all surfaces of flowerpots and saucers and allow to dry prior to painting pots. Basecoat the pots in the color that you want to be stripes and/or dots and allow to dry. If you want the terra cotta color to show through, no basecoat is required.

Place dots and rubber bands on the pots and saucers where desired. Run your finger over the edges of the dots to make sure edges are firmly affixed. Carefully brush on your topcoat of paint, making sure not to dislodge the dots. Two coats of paint may be required for good coverage. Be sure to paint both the inside and outside of the saucer as it will be used as both a lid and a saucer. When dry, carefully remove dots and rubber bands.

For the tan pot, position rubber bands as desired on terra cotta pot. Using the rubber bands as your guides, paint wide stripes on the terra cotta pot. The rubber bands will provide a nice straight edge for the stripes.

When paint is thoroughly dry, spray flowerpots and saucers inside and out with several coats of matte outdoor varnish, allowing to dry between coats.

Fill flowerpots with seed packets, flower bulbs, fertilizer sticks, gardening gloves, pruning shears, and other gardening essentials. Place saucer on top of flowerpot to form a lid and decorate with raffia, twine, or suede string.

LAYERING AND FINISHING

1. Arrange and baste backing, batting, and top together referring to Layering the Quilt directions on page 110.

2. Hand or machine quilt as desired.

3. Sew 2³/4" x 42" binding strips end to end to make one continuous 2³/4"-wide binding strip. Refer to Binding the Quilt directions on page 111 and bind quilt to finish.

4. Referring to Making Yo-yo and Circle Templates on page107, make nine yo-yos using 4¹/2" Circle Template and three using 4" Circle Template from assorted red hollyhock fabrics.

5. Referring to quilt layout on page 31 and photo on page 29, arrange and stitch hollyhock yo-yos to quilt along stalks.

6. Referring to Cat Face Template and Embroidery Stitch Guide on page 108, use two strands of embroidery floss and stem stitch to embroider cat mouth and tail, satin stitch to embroider nose, and use French knots for eyes. Sew ³/4" button to center of wheel.

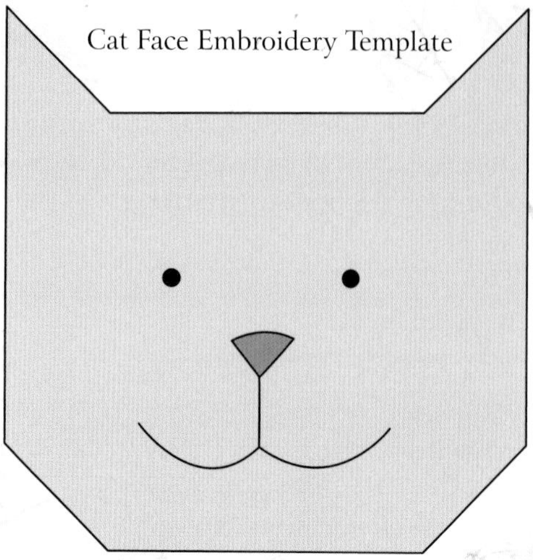

Tracing Line _____

Tracing Line _ _ _ _ _ _ _ _ _ _ _ _ _
(will be hidden behind other fabrics)

Cat Face Embroidery Template

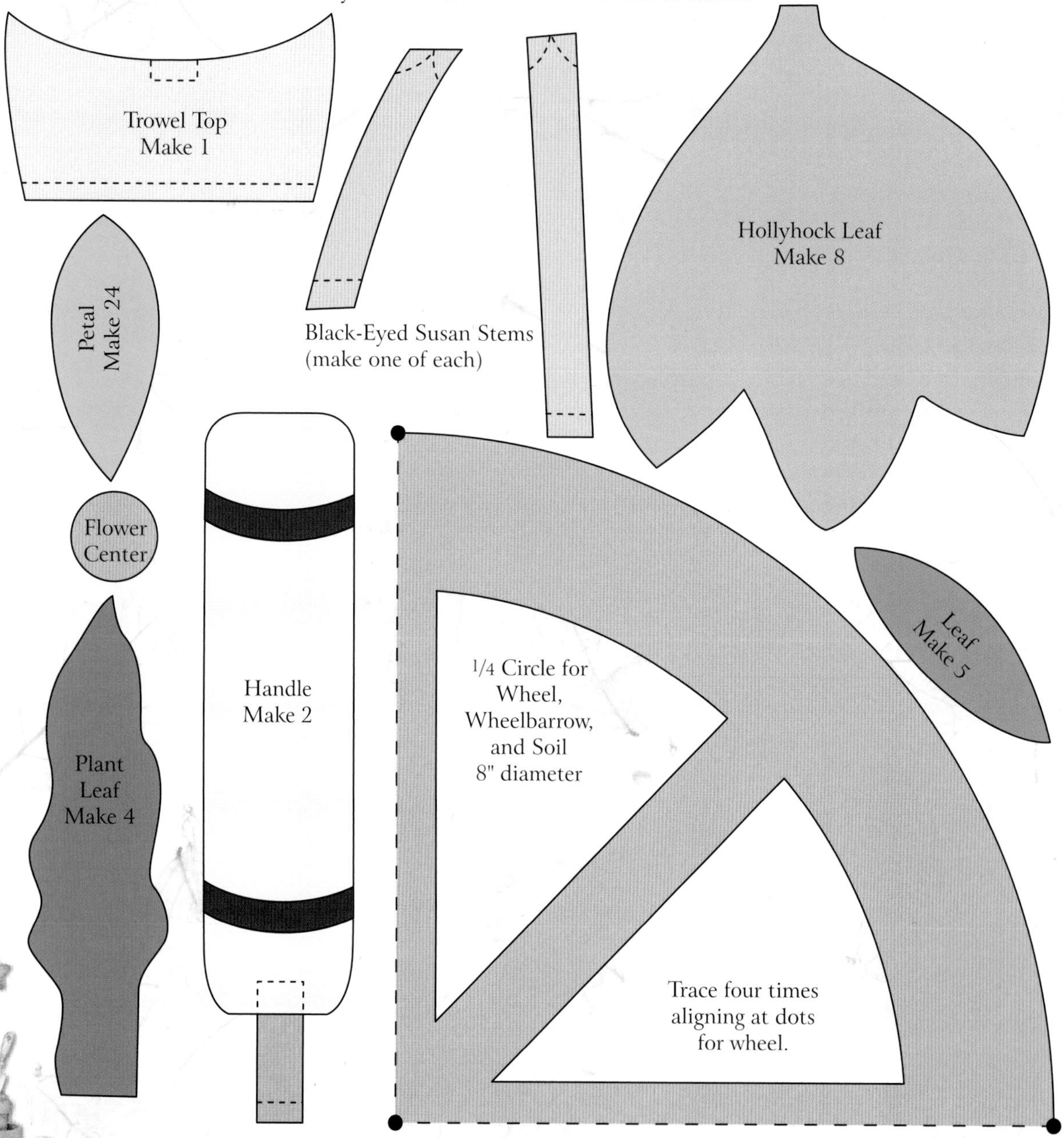

Trowel Top
Make 1

Petal
Make 24

Black-Eyed Susan Stems
(make one of each)

Hollyhock Leaf
Make 8

Flower
Center

Handle
Make 2

Plant
Leaf
Make 4

¹/4 Circle for
Wheel,
Wheelbarrow,
and Soil
8" diameter

Leaf
Make 5

Trace four times
aligning at dots
for wheel.

April Block of the Month Anemone (Right Center) Garden Glories Quilt photo on page 10		
FIRST CUT		
	Number of Strips or Pieces	Dimensions
Fabric A Background 1/8 yard	4	2 1/2" squares
	4	1 1/2" × 2"
	12	1 1/2" squares
	8	1" × 2 1/2"
Fabric B Dark Petals 1/8 yard	8	2 1/2" squares
	4	1 1/2" squares
Fabric C Light Petals 1/8 yard	4	2 1/2" squares
	4	2" × 2 1/2"
	4	1 1/2" × 2"
	4	1 1/2" squares
Fabric D Center Scrap	2	3 1/2" circle
	1	2 1/2" square
1 1/8" Button		

Assembly

1. Referring to Quick Corner Triangles on page 108, sew two 1 1/2" Fabric A squares to one 2 1/2" Fabric B square as shown. Press. Make four.

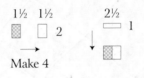

A = 1½ x 1½
B = 2½ x 2½
Make 4

2. Making quick corner triangles, sew 1 1/2" Fabric A square to 2" × 2 1/2" Fabric C piece as shown. Press. Sew unit to 1" × 2 1/2" Fabric A piece. Press. Make four.

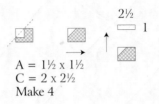

A = 1½ x 1½
C = 2 x 2½
Make 4

3. Sew 1 1/2" × 2" Fabric A and 1 1/2" × 2" Fabric C pieces together. Press. Sew unit to 1" × 2 1/2" Fabric A piece as shown. Press. Make four.

1½ 1½   2½
Make 4

4. Making quick corner triangle units, sew 1 1/2" Fabric C square to 2 1/2" Fabric B square. Sew 1 1/2" Fabric B square to 2 1/2" Fabric C square. Press. Make four of each color combination.

C = 1½ x 1½   B = 1½ x 1½
B = 2½ x 2½   C = 2½ x 2½
Make 4 of
each color
combination

5. Sew two 2 1/2" Fabric A squares and one of each unit from steps 1, 2, and 3 as shown to make a row. Press. Make two.

2½   2½
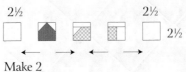
Make 2

6. Sew one unit each from steps 1 and 3 to three units from step 4 as shown to make a row. Press. Make two.

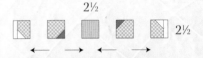
Make 2

7. Sew two units from step 2, two units from step 4, and one 2 1/2" Fabric D square as shown to make a row. Press.

2½
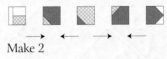

8. Sew rows together in the order shown. Press. Block measures 10 1/2" square.

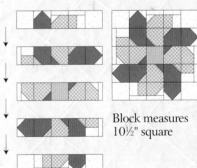

Block measures
10½" square

9. With right sides together, stitch around the edge of 3 1/2" Fabric D circles (page 107) with a 1/4" seam allowance. Clip curve and slit back side of one circle; turn right side out. Press. Run a gathering stitch making a 3/4" diameter circle in center of Fabric D circle. Gather slightly to give a wavy look to the circle, and tie off gathering threads. After quilting is completed, tack to the center of the block. Sew a button to the center of the gathered circle, through all layers.

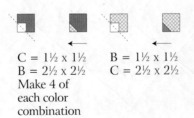

May 20
The birds twitter and flutter on the birdbath
bringing soft sounds to my garden this
morning. The last of the tulips
nod in the breeze providing a
colorful accompaniment to the
bird's chatter. It is so nice to
sit here with my morning tea enjoying
the relaxing serenity of my peaceful garden.

A birdbath ready for a feathered friend

Robin Eggs

Petite Fleur

Sitting here this morning reminds
me of a poem I learned as a child~
"Yes! in the poor man's garden grow,
Far more than herbs and flowers~
Kind thoughts, contentment, peace of mind,
And joy for weary hours."
~Mary Howitt

Checklist
☑ Prune early-flowering
   shrubs

☐ Start planting annuals

☑ Fertilize lawn

☑ Stake tall plants

~Tulips~
Sometimes called
"lipsticks of the
garden" because
they provide a finishing
touch that brings spring borders to life.

Nodding in
the breeze

PEACEFUL GARDEN

34½" SQUARE WALL QUILT

Bring the peace and serenity of the garden inside your home with this beautiful wall quilt. Easy step-by-step instructions make piecing the tulips and birdbath so quick and simple that you'll have plenty of time left to relax in the garden!

FABRIC REQUIREMENTS AND CUTTING INSTRUCTIONS

Read all instructions before beginning and use $1/4$"-wide seam allowances throughout. Read Cutting the Strips and Pieces on page 108 prior to cutting fabrics.

Peaceful Garden Wall Quilt 34$1/2$" x 34$1/2$"		
	FIRST CUT	
	Number of Strips or Pieces	Dimensions
Fabric A **Background** $1/2$ yard	1	7" square
	1	6$1/8$" square
	2	4$1/2$" x 4$3/4$"
	1	4$1/8$" square
	1	4" x 9$1/2$"
	2	4" x 2$1/2$"
	2	4" x 1$1/2$"
	2	3$1/2$" x 1$1/4$"
	4	3$1/2$" x 1"
	1	3" square
	2	2$1/2$" squares
	4	2$1/4$" x 3$1/2$"
	2	2$1/4$" x 2$1/2$"
	4	2" squares
	2	1$3/4$" x 2$1/2$"
	2	1$1/2$" x 2$1/4$"
	2	1$1/2$" x 2"
	2	1$1/2$" x 1$3/4$"
	8	1$1/2$" squares
	10	1$1/4$" squares
	2	1" x 2$1/2$"
	2	1" x 1$1/2$"
	26	1" squares
	4	$7/8$" squares
Fabric B **Birdbath** $1/8$ yard	1	2$1/2$" square
	1	2" x 7$1/2$"
	1	1$1/2$" x 3$1/2$"
	2	1$1/2$" x 2$1/2$"
	4	1" x 2$1/2$"
	4	1" squares
Fabric C **Birdbath** **Accents** *Assorted scraps*	1	9$1/2$" x 1$1/4$"
	1	3$1/2$" x 1$1/4$"
	1	2$1/2$" x 1$1/2$"
	2	1$1/2$" x 5$1/2$"
	2	1$1/2$" squares
Fabric D **Ground** *Scrap*	1	5" square

Peaceful Garden Wall Quilt Continued		
	FIRST CUT	
	Number of Strips or Pieces	Dimensions
Fabric E Tulip *Assorted Scraps*	1*	2$1/2$" x 3$1/2$"
	2*	1" x 3"
	2*	1" squares
	*cut for each of two tulips	
Fabric F **Ruffle Tulip** *Assorted Scraps*	1*	2$1/2$" x 3$1/2$"
	2*	1" x 2$1/2$"
	2*	1" x 1$1/2$"
	2*	1" squares
	*cut for each of two tulips	
Fabric G **Leaves and** **Stems** *Assorted Scraps*	8	2$1/4$" squares
	2	1" x 3$1/2$"
	2	1" x 2$1/2$"
	2	1" x 1$1/2$"
BORDERS		
Accent **Border** $1/6$ yard	2	1$1/2$" x 17$3/4$"
	2	1$1/2$" x 19$3/4$"
Corner **Triangles** $1/2$ yard	2	14$1/2$" squares
First Border $1/4$ yard	4	1$1/4$" x 42"
Outside **Border** $1/3$ yard	4	2$1/2$" x 42"
Binding $3/8$ yard	4	2$3/4$" x 42"

Bird Appliqué - Assorted scraps
Backing - 1$1/8$ yards
Batting - 40" x 40"
Lightweight Fusible Web - Scraps

MAKING THE BLOCKS

You will be making two each of two different tulip blocks. Each tulip is made in a different color. Whenever possible, use the Assembly Line Method on page 108. Press in the direction of arrows.

ASSEMBLY

1. Referring to Quick Corner Triangles on page 108, sew two 1$1/2$" Fabric A and two 1" Fabric E squares to 2$1/2$" x 3$1/2$" Fabric E piece as shown.

A = 1½ x 1½
E = 1 x 1
2½ x 3½

2. Making quick corner triangle units, sew two 1" Fabric A squares to 1" x 3" Fabric E piece as shown. Press. Sew 1" Fabric A square to this unit as shown. Press. Make two, one of each variation.

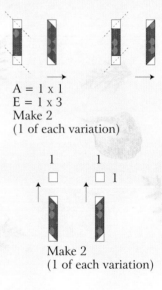

A = 1 x 1
E = 1 x 3
Make 2
(1 of each variation)

Make 2
(1 of each variation)

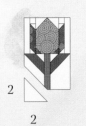

3. Arrange and sew unit from step 1, units from step 2, and two 3½" x 1" Fabric A pieces as shown. Press.

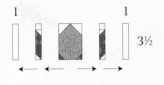

4. Making quick corner triangle units, sew 2¼" Fabric G square to 2¼" x 3½" Fabric A piece as shown. Press. Sew 1¼" Fabric A square to this unit as shown. Press. Make two, one of each variation.

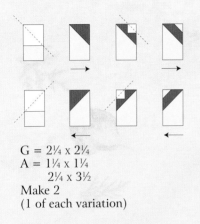

G = 2¼ x 2¼
A = 1¼ x 1¼
    2¼ x 3½
Make 2
(1 of each variation)

5. Sew 1" x 3½" Fabric G piece between units from step 4 as shown. Press.

6. Sew unit from step 3 to unit from step 5 as shown. Press. Repeat steps 1-6 to make another tulip block in a different color combination.

7. Measure and mark 2" on both sides of corner of first unit from step 6. Align cutting guide at marks and cut off corner as shown. Repeat for second unit as shown.

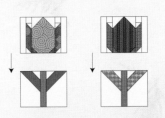

Blooming Daisy

Peaceful Garden Wall Quilt
Finished Size: 34½" x 34½"; Photo: page 37

8. Measure and mark 7/8" on both sides of corner of 4 1/2" x 4 3/4" Fabric A piece as shown. Matching marks as you did in step 7, trim. These sides now measure 3 5/8" and 3 7/8" from corner to cut. Repeat for second Fabric A square as shown.

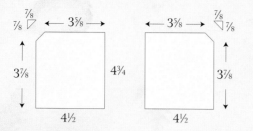

9. Cut 4 1/8" and 3" Fabric A squares in half once diagonally. Arrange and sew together triangles, piece from step 8, and unit from step 7 as shown to make a row. Press. Repeat for second row. Press.

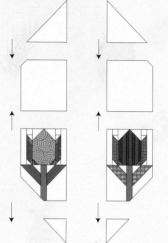

10. Cut 6 1/8" Fabric A square in half once diagonally. Sew triangles to sides of units from step 9 as shown. Press.

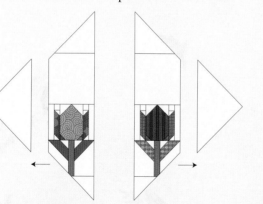

11. Making quick corner triangle units, sew two 1 1/2" Fabric A and two 1" Fabric F squares to 2 1/2" x 3 1/2" Fabric F piece as shown. Press. Make two, one of each tulip color combination.

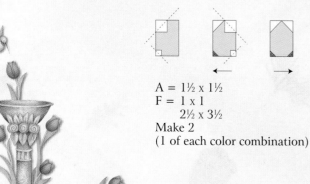

A = 1 1/2 x 1 1/2
F = 1 x 1
    2 1/2 x 3 1/2
Make 2
(1 of each color combination)

12. Making quick corner triangle units, sew two 1" Fabric A squares to 1" x 1 1/2" Fabric F piece as shown. Press. Make two, one of each variation.

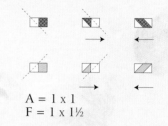

A = 1 x 1
F = 1 x 1 1/2

13. Making quick corner triangle units, sew 1" Fabric A and 1" Fabric B squares to 1" x 1 1/2" Fabric F piece as shown. Press. Make two, one of each variation.

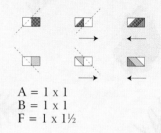

A = 1 x 1
B = 1 x 1
F = 1 x 1 1/2

14. Sew 1" Fabric A and 1" Fabric B squares together. Press. Make two. Sew to units from step 13 as shown. Sew 1" x 1 1/2" Fabric A piece to units from step 12 as shown. Press.

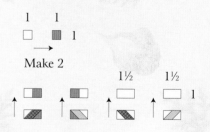

15. Making quick corner triangle units, sew 1" Fabric A square to 1" x 2 1/2" Fabric F piece. Press. Make four, two variations of each color as shown.

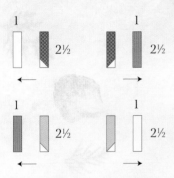

A = 1 x 1
F = 1 x 2½

16. Sew units from step 15 to 1" x 2 1/2" Fabric A and Fabric B pieces as shown. Press.

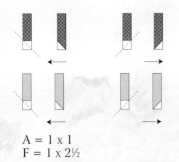

17. Sew units from step 14 to units from step 16 as shown. Press.

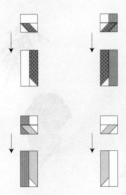

18. Sew unit from step 11 between two units from step 17 as shown. Press. Make two, one of each color combination.

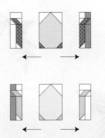

19. Sew 1" x 2 1/2" Fabric B piece to 1 3/4" x 2 1/2" Fabric A piece. Press. Make two.

1   1¾

2½

Make 2

20. Making quick corner triangle units, sew 2 1/4" Fabric G squares to 2 1/4" x 2 1/2" Fabric A pieces, and units from step 19 as shown. Press. Make four, one of each variation.

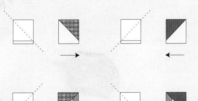

G = 2¼ x 2¼
A = 2¼ x 2½
Make 4
(1 of each variation)

21. Making quick corner triangle units, sew 1 1/4" Fabric A squares to units from step 20 as shown. Press. Make four, one of each variation.

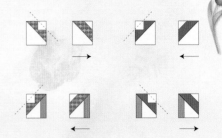

A = 1¼ x 1¼
Make 4
(1 of each variation)

22. Sew 1" x 2 1/2" Fabric G piece between units from step 21 as shown. Press. Make two, one of each variation.

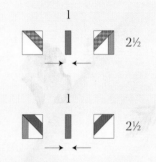

1

2½

1

2½

23. Making quick corner triangle units, sew 1 1/2" Fabric C square to 1 1/2" x 1 3/4" Fabric A piece as shown. Press. Make two, one of each variation.

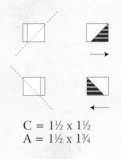

C = 1½ x 1½
A = 1½ x 1¾

Tender Tulip

24. Sew 1" x 1½" Fabric G piece between 1½" x 2¼" Fabric A piece and unit from step 23 as shown. Press. Make two, one of each variation.

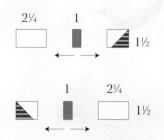

25. Sew 1½" x 3½" Fabric B piece between units from step 18; 1½" x 2½" Fabric B piece between units from step 22; and 2½" x 1½" Fabric C piece between units from step 24 into rows as shown. Press. Sew rows together. Press.

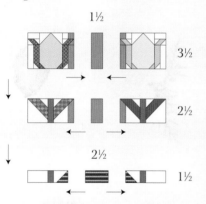

26. On unit from step 25, measure and mark 1¾" on both sides of lower corners as shown. Align cutting guide at marks and cut off corners.

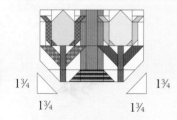

27. Making quick corner triangle units, sew two 1¼" Fabric A squares to 9½" x 1¼" Fabric C piece as shown. Press.

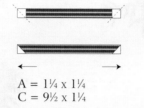

A = 1¼ x 1¼
C = 9½ x 1¼

28. Making quick corner triangle units, sew two 2" Fabric A squares to 2" x 7½" Fabric B piece as shown. Press. Sew unit between two 1½" x 2" Fabric A pieces. Press.

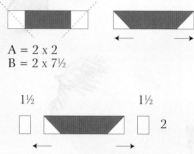

A = 2 x 2
B = 2 x 7½

29. Sew two different 1½" x 5½" Fabric C pieces together as shown. Making quick corner triangle units, sew two 1" and two 2" Fabric A squares to unit as shown. Press.

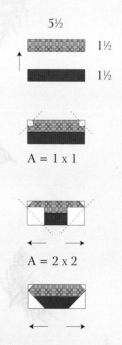

A = 1 x 1

A = 2 x 2

30. Sew unit from step 29 between two 2½" Fabric A squares. Sew 2½" Fabric B square between two 4" x 2½" Fabric A pieces as shown. Press.

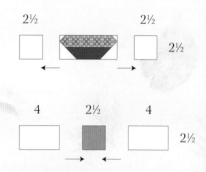

31. Making quick corner triangle units, sew four ⅞" Fabric A squares to 3½" x 1¼" Fabric C piece as shown. Press. Sew unit between two 3½" x 1¼" Fabric A pieces. Press.

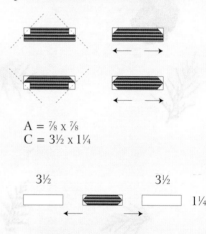

A = ⅞ x ⅞
C = 3½ x 1¼

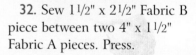

32. Sew 1½" x 2½" Fabric B piece between two 4" x 1½" Fabric A pieces. Press.

Black-Eyed Susan

33. Cut 7" Fabric A and 5" Fabric D squares each in half once diagonally (you will have one triangle of each color left over). Sew triangles, 4" x 9½" Fabric A piece and units from steps 26 through 32 together as shown. Press.

9½

4

Painted Pot Birdbath

The birds will love this one-of-a-kind birdbath made from inexpensive terra cotta flowerpots. Easy painting techniques in sumptuous spring colors will make this birdbath the centerpiece of your garden.

Materials Needed:

Three terra cotta pots in graduated sizes
(When purchasing pots, stack them upside down, one on top of the other, to get a height and look that you like)
Large terra cotta saucer
(Look for a saucer that is glazed on the inside so that it will hold water)
Sea sponge and stencils
Scotch® Magic™ Tape
All-purpose sealer
Acrylic paints and paint brushes
Marine varnish

Following manufacturer's directions, apply all-purpose sealer to surfaces to be painted. Allow to dry. Apply basecoat colors. This will generally require two coats for complete coverage. When dry, sponge on a slightly darker color to one or more of the pots, if desired. Draw stripes and checks on with a ruler and pencil to help keep lines straight. A checkerboard stencil can also be used to paint checks. Scotch® Magic™ Tape can be used to mask areas and to keep straight lines. On areas where checks or stripes are painted, apply lightest color first, then paint stripes or checks over lighter base color. Add squiggles, dots, vines, and leaves as desired.

When completely dry, apply marine varnish according to manufacturer's directions. We did not permanently glue our pots together so that we can dismantle the birdbath in winter and store the pots one inside the other in a sheltered area.

34. Sew units from step 10 to each side of unit from step 33. Press. Block measures 17¾" square. *(This completes the May Block of the Month center panel).*

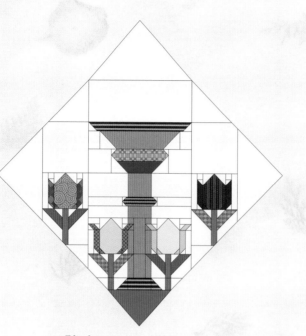

Block measures 17¾" square

BORDERS FOR WALL QUILT

1. Sew 1½" x 17¾" Accent Border strips to opposite sides of center panel. Press seams toward border strips. Sew 1½" x 19¾" Accent Border strips to remaining sides. Press.

2. Cut 14½" Corner Triangle squares in half once diagonally to make two sets of two triangles. When using directional fabric, make diagonal cuts in opposite directions. Referring to quilt layout on page 39, sew one triangle to each side of unit from step 1. Press toward triangles. Square quilt if necessary to measure 28½" square.

3. Measure quilt through center from side to side. Cut two 1¼" x 42" First Border strips to this measurement. Sew to opposite sides. Press seams toward borders.

4. Measure quilt through center from side to side including borders just added. Cut remaining 1¼"-wide strips to this measurement. Sew to remaining sides. Press.

5. Repeat steps 3 and 4 to fit, trim, and sew 2½"-wide Outside Borders to all sides. Press.

ADDING THE APPLIQUÉS

The instructions given are for the Quick-Fuse Appliqué method. If you prefer traditional hand appliqué, be sure to reverse all appliqué templates and add ¼" seam allowances when cutting appliqué pieces. Refer to Hand Appliqué on page 109.

1. Referring to Quick-Fuse Appliqué directions on page 109, trace bird appliqués from templates on page 26.

2. Refer to layout on page 39 and photo on page 37. Position and fuse bird in place and finish with machine satin stitch or decorative stitching as desired.

LAYERING AND FINISHING

1. Layer backing, batting, and top together, referring to Layering the Quilt directions on page 110.

2. Machine or hand quilt as desired.

3. Refer to Binding the Quilt directions on page 111 and use 2¾" x 42" binding strips to finish.

Entries

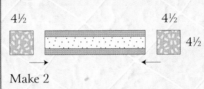

May Block of the Month
Birdbath and Borders

For Birdbath Center Panel, refer to cutting chart on page 38.
Garden Glories Quilt photo on page 10

BORDERS		
	Number of Strips or Pieces	Dimensions
Sashing 1/4 yard	4	1 1/2" x 42"
Center/First Border 1/4 yard	2	2 1/2" x 42"
Cornerstones 1/6 yard	4	4 1/2" squares

Assembly

Refer to Peaceful Garden Wall Quilt steps 1-34 on pages 38-44 to make one 17 3/4" square center panel.

1. Sew 2 1/2" x 42" Center/First Border strip between 1 1/2" x 42" Sashing strips. Press. Make two. Cut strip sets into four 17 3/4" segments.

42

1 1/2

2 1/2

1 1/2

Make 2
(cut four 17 3/4" segments)

2. Sew unit from step 1 between two 4 1/2" Cornerstone squares. Press. Make two.

4 1/2   4 1/2

4 1/2

Make 2

3. Sew center panel between two units from step 1. Press toward sashing. Sew this unit between two units from step 2. Press. Block measures 25 3/4" square.

Tracing Line _____

Tracing Line _ _ _ _ _ _ _ _ _ _ _ _
(will be hidden behind other fabrics)

Embroidery Line _ _ _ _ _ _ _ _ _ _

4. Refer to Quick-Fuse Appliqué directions on page 109. Trace hummingbird pattern. Referring to photo for placement, arrange and fuse appliqués to quilt. Referring to Machine Appliqué on page 109, finish edges with machine satin stitch or decorative stitching as desired. Refer to Embroidery Stitch Guide on page 108 to add French knot for hummingbird eye and satin stitch for the beak.

Hummingbird for May Block
Quick-Fuse Pattern

*Appliqué pattern is reversed for use with
Quick-Fuse Appliqué
(page 109)*

Fanciful Floral Stamps

June 23
It's been several days since I last wrote in this journal...I hate to miss a day, the garden changes so quickly! Added a few more pansies to the shade beds near the house. I love the pansies' sweet whiskered faces!

White Pansies

Pretty Daisy

Pansies~
~Bloom until frost
~Little cat-faced flowers
~Great for borders and pots
~Like shade in the afternoons

Purple Tiger Pansy

Found this quotation in one of my gardening books ... really describes how I feel~

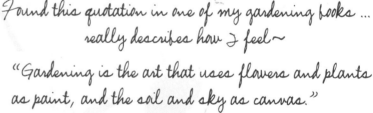

"Gardening is the art that uses flowers and plants as paint, and the soil and sky as canvas."
~Elizabeth Murray

Daisies in Bloom

a quick sketch

Beautiful Sunflower

Fiddlehead fern

GARDEN JOURNAL AND PANSY TOTE

Record all your garden musings in this beautiful wooden journal decorated with vintage seed packets and pressed flowers. The journal will fit inside the pocket of this indispensable tool tote embellished with easy stamped images of pansies, ferns, and dragonflies.

Garden Journal

4. To achieve a distressed finish, sand the edges of the journal cover so the wood shows through. Next, sand the center area to soften the green and allow the white to show through. Following manufacturer's instructions, apply antiquing gel over the whole painted surface, then rub off until desired color is achieved. The journal cover will be darker on the areas where the wood shows through. Mix water with black paint and fill an old toothbrush with the watered-down paint. Rub thumb over the bristles to add black paint spatters to the journal cover. We suggest that you practice this technique on a piece of paper before trying it on your journal cover. If spatters are too heavy or large, use a cotton swab to remove unwanted splatters before the paint dries. Allow cover to dry completely.

MATERIALS NEEDED:

Wooden journal (available at
   craft supply stores)
Wood sealer
Pressed flowers (See page 49)
Vintage Seed packets*
Découpage glue
Glass beads
24-gauge brass wire
Leather string
Crackle medium
Watercolor paper
Rusted-tin decorative banner
Matte spray varnish
Acrylic paints: black, antique
   white, medium green
Dark brown antiquing gel
E6000® glue
Assorted brushes

* Available from
NK Lawn and Garden
3701 Amnicola Highway
Chattanooga, TN 37406
(800) 848-6290

INSTRUCTIONS:

1. Take journal apart and remove the hardware.

2. Seal all the wooden areas following manufacturer's directions. Dry completely, then sand until smooth.

3. Paint the front of the journal antique white. When dry, lightly sponge the center area of the journal with medium green, referring to photo above. Allow to dry completely.

5. Determine the placement of the banner, seed packets, pressed flowers, and foliage by laying them on the journal cover. Do not start gluing until the various elements have been placed as desired. Following manufacturer's directions on the découpage glue, begin gluing elements to the cover, making sure that items underneath other pieces are glued first. Pressed flowers tear very easily so apply the découpage carefully. When the first coat of découpage is dry, add another coat to the entire surface.

6. Using a purchased rusted-tin banner as the background, tear a piece of watercolor paper to fit on top of the banner. Distress the watercolor paper by wetting it and applying a little of the antique white paint and some antiquing gel to the edges. When dry, spatter with black paint. When spatters are dry, paint or stencil the words "Garden Journal."

7. Glue the painted watercolor paper on the banner then glue the banner to the journal. A heavy-duty glue such as E6000® will be needed to affix the banner. Two decorative beads were glued over the holes on the banner.

8. Paint the back and the binding edge of the journal black. When dry, apply crackle medium according to manufacturer's instructions. When crackle medium has "set" according to the instructions, paint surfaces with medium green to create the crackle.

9. When dry, spray two coats of a matte spray varnish over all the painted and decoupaged areas. Reassemble journal.

10. Rather than use the posts provided, we chose to use a leather string to bind our journal. Use a fine gold-colored wire and attach glass beads to the leather string. Wrap the wire around the beads creating a wire-and-bead design. Just tie the leather string at the back of the journal. Pages can be easily changed and added to the journal with this easy binding method.

Pressing Flowers and Leaves

Hobby stores offer a variety of flower presses, including ones that can be used in microwave ovens. Flower presses are also easy to make using peg board, blotter paper, and screws with wing nuts. Look for directions on how to make a flower press on the Internet or in hobby books. We pressed most of our flowers and leaves by carefully positioning them in old telephone books. It took a little longer for items to thoroughly dry, but the results were excellent. We left our flowers in the telephone book for one week, two weeks for leaves. If you live in an area with high humidity, it may take longer. Flowers and leaves will be brittle when they are thoroughly dried.

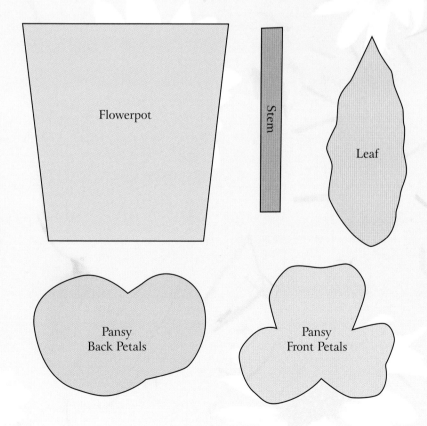

GARDEN JOURNAL

Flowerpot

Stem

Leaf

Pansy Back Petals

Pansy Front Petals

Pansy Tote Sponge-Stamping Shapes

Pansy Tote

MATERIALS NEEDED:

Canvas tote
Miracle Sponge™ or purchased
   fabric stamps*
Ruler
Acrylic paint: golden yellow,
   dark purple, black,
   terra cotta, medium green,
   medium tan
Fabric medium
Disposable palette paper (or
   paper plate)
Sharp craft scissors
Coffee (make double strength)
Spray bottles

*Miracle Sponge™ is thinly
compressed cellulose that can
be cut with scissors and
expands when wet. It is
available at many arts and
crafts supply stores.

INSTRUCTIONS:

1. To give tote a vintage
appearance, use coffee to stain
it. Dampen the bag with a
misting of clear water. While
still wet, spray the bag with the
coffee solution until a desired
stained look appears. (You may
want to do this step outside!)
Let dry thoroughly.

2. Most of the shapes for
stamping were cut from Miracle
Sponge™. Use the artwork on
seed packets for inspiration, or
use appliqué shapes from this
book for flowers and insects.
The pansy and flowerpot
shapes featured on our tote are
on page 49, but may need to be
resized depending on your tote.
The checks were cut from
Miracle Sponge™ using a ruler
to measure the desired square
shape. The dragonfly shape was
cut from Miracle Sponge™
using the appliqué template on
page 61. The fern shape is a
purchased stamp. There are
many stamp shapes that can
be purchased to use on your
tote in a wide variety of
garden themes.

3. Place a small amount of
paint on palette paper and add
a few drops of fabric medium,
following the manufacturer's
instructions on the bottle for
amount to mix. Dampen
sponge shape and wring out
well. Dip sponge into the paint
so the whole surface of the
sponge is covered. Apply to the
bag. We recommend practicing
on a piece of cloth before
applying shapes to the tote.
Allow to dry completely.

4. Heat-set painted tote
with a hot dry iron and a
pressing cloth.

Sunny faces!

June Block of the Month Daisy (Top Center) Garden Glories Quilt photo on page 10		
FIRST CUT		
	Number of Strips or Pieces	Dimensions
Fabric A Background *1/8 yard*	2	3 1/2" squares
	2	2" x 5 1/2"
	2	2" x 4"
	4	2" squares
	4	1 1/2" squares
Fabric B Daisy *Assorted scraps of three fabrics*	2	4" squares
	4	2 1/2" x 3 1/2"
	4	2 1/2" squares
Fabric C Center *Scrap*	1	5 1/2" circle
1" Button		

Assembly

1. Referring to Quick Corner Triangles on page 108, sew 1 1/2" Fabric A square to 2 1/2" x 3 1/2" Fabric B piece as shown. Press. Make four, two of each variation.

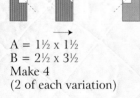

A = 1½ x 1½
B = 2½ x 3½
Make 4
(2 of each variation)

2. Sew unit from step 1 to 3 1/2" Fabric A square as shown. Press. Make two.

3 1/2

3 1/2

Make 2

3. Making quick corner triangle units, sew two 2 1/2" Fabric B squares together as shown. Press. Make two.

B = 2½ x 2½
2½ x 2½
Make 2

4. Sew unit from step 1 to unit from step 3 as shown. Press. Make two.

Make 2

5. Sew unit from step 2 to unit from step 4 as shown. Press. Make two.

Make 2

6. Making quick corner triangle units, sew two 2" Fabric A squares to opposite corners of 4" Fabric B square. Press. Make two.

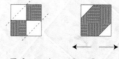

Fabric A = 2 x 2
Fabric B = 4 x 4
Make 2

7. Sew 2" x 4" Fabric A piece to unit from step 6. Press. Sew 2" x 5 1/2" Fabric A piece to side of unit as shown. Press. Make 2.

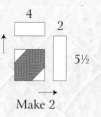

4

2

5½

Make 2

8. Sew unit from step 5 to unit from step 7. Press. Make two. Sew units together. Press. Block measures 10 1/2" square.

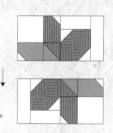

Make 2

Block measures 10½" square

9. Using the 5 1/2"-Circle Template, make center yo-yo following the directions on page 107. After quilting is completed, sew yo-yo and button to center of flower.

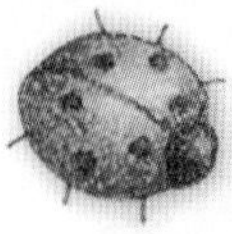

July 18
A ladybug just landed on my hand. I'm sure glad to see these helpful critters near my roses!

Mint Leaf

Green Bug Lunch

Bright colors invite bug friends!

A praying mantis lives beside the patio and the whole family has been entertained by this strange-looking fellow. We've nicknamed him Mickey Mantis.

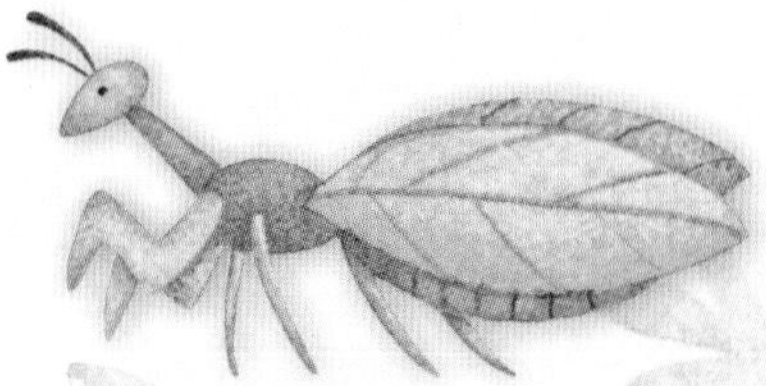

Beneficial bugs:
~ Ladybug Beetles
~ Praying mantis
~ Green lacewing
Protect my flowers from bad bugs!

Pretty Posies

This time of the year the yard is alive with flowers and butterflies! It's a joy to watch the butterflies land on the beautiful blossoms.

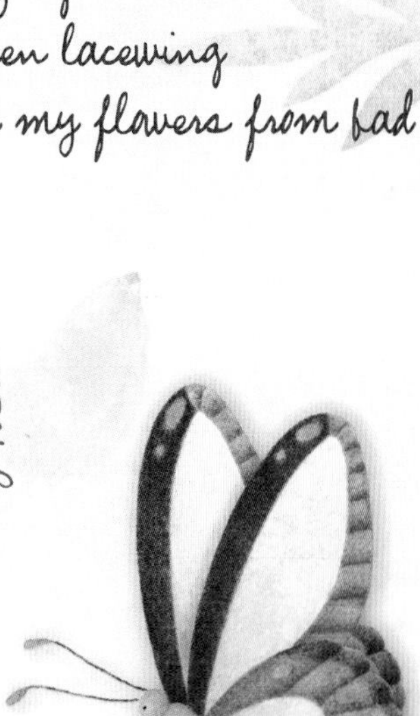

Vibrant Butterfly

BUG LOVE

69" x 85" BED QUILT

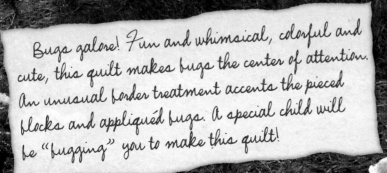

Bugs galore! Fun and whimsical, colorful and cute, this quilt makes bugs the center of attention. An unusual border treatment accents the pieced blocks and appliquéd bugs. A special child will be "bugging" you to make this quilt!

FABRIC REQUIREMENTS AND CUTTING INSTRUCTIONS

Read all instructions before beginning and use 1/4"-wide seam allowances throughout. Read Cutting the Strips and Pieces on page 108 prior to cutting fabrics.

Bug Love Bed Quilt 69" x 85"	FIRST CUT		SECOND CUT	
	Number of Strips or Pieces	Dimensions	Number of Pieces	Dimensions
BUG BLOCK				
Fabric A Yellow Background 5/8 yard (directional)**	3	4 1/2" x 42"	16 16	4 1/2" squares 4 1/2" x 2 1/2"
	2	2 1/2" x 42"	16	2 1/2" x 4 1/2"
Fabric A Blue Background 7/8 yard	6	4 1/2" x 42"	24 48	4 1/2" squares 4 1/2" x 2 1/2"
Fabric A Orange Background 1/3 yard	2	4 1/2" x 42"	8 16	4 1/2" squares 4 1/2" x 2 1/2"
Fabric B Octagon Border 1/3 yard*	3*	2 1/2" x 42" *cut for each of six fabrics*	40*	2 1/2" squares
Fabric C Diamond Border 7/8 yard*	11*	2 1/2" x 42" *cut for each of two fabrics*	48* 72*	2 1/2" x 4 1/2" 2 1/2" squares
Fabric D Bug Background 1/6 yard*	1*	4 1/2" x 42" *cut for each of six fabrics*	8*	4 1/2" squares
BORDERS				
First Border 1/2 yard	6	2 1/2" x 42"	4	2 1/2" squares
Second Border 7/8 yard	1 6	5 1/2" x 42" 3 1/2" x 42"	4	5 1/2" squares
Third Border 1/2 yard	1 6	6 1/2" x 42" 1 1/2" x 42"	4	6 1/2" squares
Outside Border 1 1/4 yards	9	4 1/2" x 42"	4	4 1/2" x 22 1/2"
Binding 2/3 yard	8	2 3/4" x 42"		

Appliqué Bugs - Assorted scraps
Backing - 5 1/8 yards
Batting - 77" x 93"
Lightweight Fusible Web - 1 yard
Embroidery Floss
**For directional fabric the measurement that is listed first runs parallel to selvage (strip width).*

MAKING THE BLOCKS

Refer to Accurate Seam Allowance on page 108 before making twelve Bug Blocks. All blocks measure 16 1/2" square, unfinished. This quilt uses three different Fabric A background pieces. We made four in yellow, six in blue, and two in orange. To give the quilt a scrappy look, we made two blocks each using six different Fabric B Octagon Border and Fabric D Bug Background fabrics. We made six blocks each of two different Fabric C Diamond Border fabrics. Use the Assembly Line Method on page 108 whenever possible. Press seams in direction of arrows.

BUG BLOCKS

Instructions given are for one Bug Block. Repeat to make twelve blocks.

1. Refer to Quick Corner Triangles on page 108. Sew 2 1/2" Fabric B square to 4 1/2" Fabric A square as shown. Press. Make four. For Fabric A, we used directional fabric. We cut out pieces and carefully placed them when piecing so the fabric pattern would be aligned correctly.

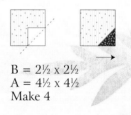

B = 2½ x 2½
A = 4½ x 4½
Make 4

2. Making a quick corner triangle unit, sew 2 1/2" Fabric C square to 4 1/2" Fabric D square as shown. Press. Make four.

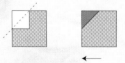

C = 2½ x 2½
D = 4½ x 4½
Make 4

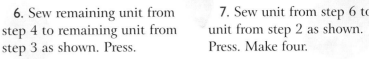

3. Making quick corner triangle units, sew two 2¹/₂" Fabric B squares to 2¹/₂" x 4¹/₂" Fabric C piece as shown. Make eight, four of each variation.

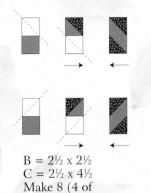

B = 2½ x 2½
C = 2½ x 4½
Make 8 (4 of
each variation)

4. Making quick corner triangle units, sew 2¹/₂" Fabric C squares to 2¹/₂" x 4¹/₂" and 4¹/₂" x 2¹/₂" Fabric A pieces as shown. Press. Make eight, four of each variation.

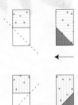

C = 2½ x 2½
A = 2½ x 4½
    4½ x 2½
Make 8
(4 of each variation)

5. Sew first unit from step 4 to first unit from step 3 as shown. Press. Make four. Sew this unit to unit from step 1 as shown. Press. Make four.

Make 4   Make 4

6. Sew remaining unit from step 4 to remaining unit from step 3 as shown. Press. Make four.

Make 4

7. Sew unit from step 6 to unit from step 2 as shown. Press. Make four.

Make 4

Beautiful Dragonfly

Bug Love Bed Quilt
Finished Size: 69" x 85"; Photo: page 53

8. Sew units from steps 5 and 7 as shown. Press. Make four.

Make 4

9. Sew units from step 8 together as shown. Press seams open. Referring to quilt layout on page 55 and photo on page 53, repeat steps 1 through 9 to make a total of twelve Bug Blocks in color variations shown. Blocks measure 16 1/2" square.

Block measures 16 1/2" square
Make 12
(4 yellow background
6 blue background
2 orange background)

Hopalong Grasshopper

ADDING THE APPLIQUÉS

The instructions given are for the Quick-Fuse Appliqué method. If you prefer traditional hand appliqué, be sure to reverse all appliqué templates and add 1/4" seam allowance when cutting appliqué pieces. Refer to Hand Appliqué on page 109.

1. Refer to Quick-Fuse Appliqué on page 109. Trace appliqué patterns on pages 58-60. Enlarge butterflies and dragonflies on page 61 to 150% and trace.

2. Referring to quilt layout on page 55 and photo on page 53, position appliqués on blocks. Fuse appliqués in place and finish with machine satin stitch or decorative stitching as desired.

ASSEMBLY

1. Refer to quilt layout on page 55 and photo on page 53. Arrange and sew blocks in four horizontal rows of three blocks each. Press seams in opposite directions from row to row.

2. Sew rows together. Press.

3. Sew 2 1/2" x 42" First Border strips together end to end to make one continuous 2 1/2"-wide strip. Repeat to sew 3 1/2"-wide Second Border and 1 1/2"-wide Third Border strips together. Press.

4. Assemble and sew the First, Second, and Third Border strips together to make a border strip set, staggering seams. Referring to Adding the Borders on page 110, measure quilt through center from side to side and top to bottom. Cut two border strip sets to each of these measurements. These measurements will be used again in step 10 for Outside Border Strips.

1 1/2

3 1/2

2 1/2

5. Referring to Quilt layout on page 55, sew short strip sets from step 4 to top and bottom of quilt. Press toward borders.

6. Making quick corner triangle units, sew 5 1/2" Second Border square to 6 1/2" Third Border square as shown. Press. Make four. Sew 2 1/2" First Border square to this unit. Press. Make four.

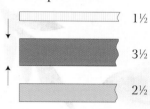

Third Border = 6 1/2 x 6 1/2
Second Border = 5 1/2 x 5 1/2
First Border = 2 1/2 x 2 1/2
Make 4

7. Draw a diagonal line from corner to corner on wrong side of square unit from step 6. Stay stitch 1/8" from drawn line. Cut 1/4" away from drawn line as shown.

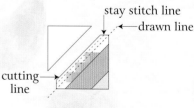

stay stitch line
drawn line
cutting line

8. Referring to Quilt layout on page 55 and photo on page 53, sew remaining long border strip sets from step 4 between two units from step 7. Press. Make two.

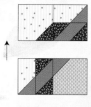

9. Sew strip sets from step 8 to sides of quilt. Press toward border.

10. Sew 4½" x 42" Outside Border strips end to end to make one continuous 4½"-wide strip. Using measurements from step 4, cut two 4½"-wide Outside Border strips to each of these measurements. Sew shorter strips to top and bottom of quilt and longer strips to sides. Press.

11. Align ruler to outside quilt edge as shown. Trim along edge of ruler.

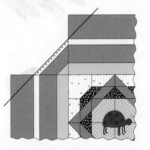

12. Sew 4½" x 22½" Outside Border to corner. Press. Aligning ruler to outside edge of quilt, trim as shown. Repeat for all corners.

ladybug

LAYERING AND BINDING

1. Cut backing crosswise into two equal pieces and sew pieces together to make one 84" x 92" (approximate) piece. Press. Cut backing to 77" x 92". Arrange and baste backing, batting, and top together, referring to Layering the Quilt on page 110.

2. Hand or machine quilt as desired.

3. Sew the 2¾" x 42" binding strips end to end to make one continuous 2¾"-wide binding strip. Refer to Binding the Quilt and Mitered Corners on page 111 and bind quilt to finish.

Bug Love Pillow Sham

Finished Size: 38" x 28"

Beautiful bugs buzz around this pillow sham, making it the perfect accent for your Bug Love Quilt!

Fabric Requirements for One Pillow Sham

Fabric A Background - (⅝ yard)
   One 20½" x 30½" piece
First Border - (⅓ yard)
   Four 2" x 42" strips
   Four 2" squares
Outside Border - (½ yard)
   Four 4½" squares
   Four 3" x 42" strips
Backing - (1⅓ yards)
   Two 22" x 28½" pieces

Making the Pillow Top

1. Sew 2" x 42" First Border strips and 3" x 42" Outside Border strips together lengthwise in pairs. Make four. Cut two 20½" and two 30½" lengths from strip sets.

2. Refer to Quick Corner Triangles on page 108. Sew one 2" First Border square to 4½" Outside Border square as shown. Press. Make four.

First Border = 2 x 2
Outside Border = 4½ x 4½
Make 4

3. Referring to pillow layout above, sew 20½" x 30½" Fabric A piece between two 30½" strip sets from step 1. Press.

4. Sew 20½" strip set from step 1 between two units from step 2. Press toward strip set. Make two.

5. Referring to pillow layout, sew unit from step 3 between two units from step 4. Press.

6. Referring to pillow layout and Adding the Appliqués for the Bug Love Bed Quilt on page 56, position and fuse appliqués in place.

7. Refer to Finishing Pillows on page 111 to quilt top and sew pillow backing to pillow.

8. Stitch-in-the ditch between the Fabric A panel and First Border to create a flange.

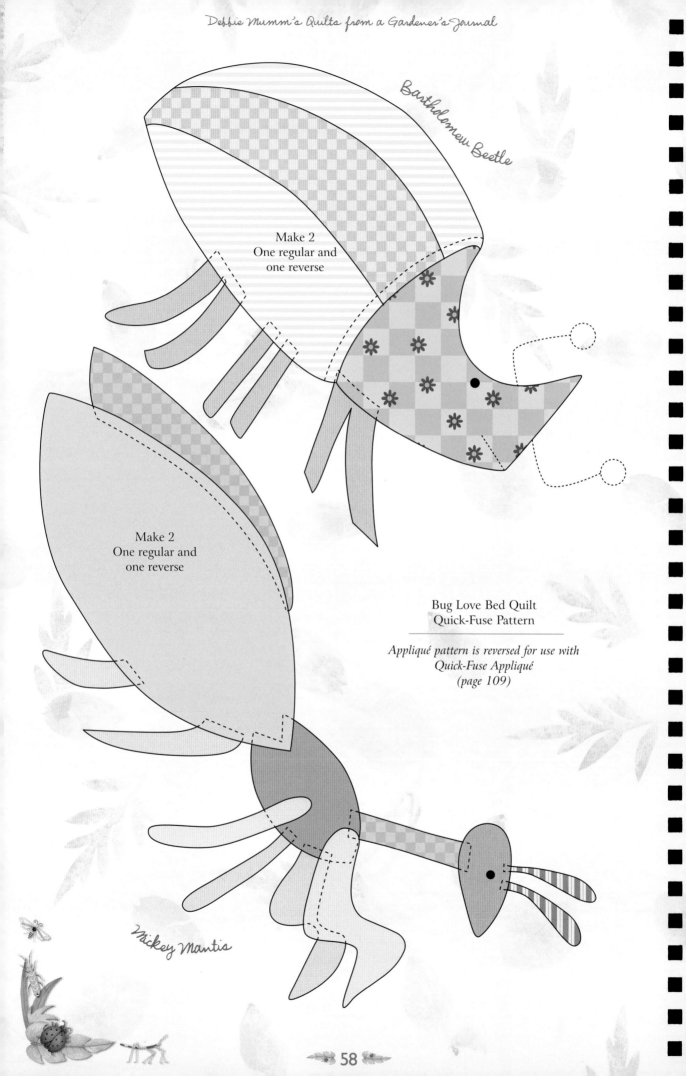

Bartholomew Beetle

Make 2
One regular and
one reverse

Make 2
One regular and
one reverse

Bug Love Bed Quilt
Quick-Fuse Pattern

*Appliqué pattern is reversed for use with
Quick-Fuse Appliqué
(page 109)*

Mickey Mantis

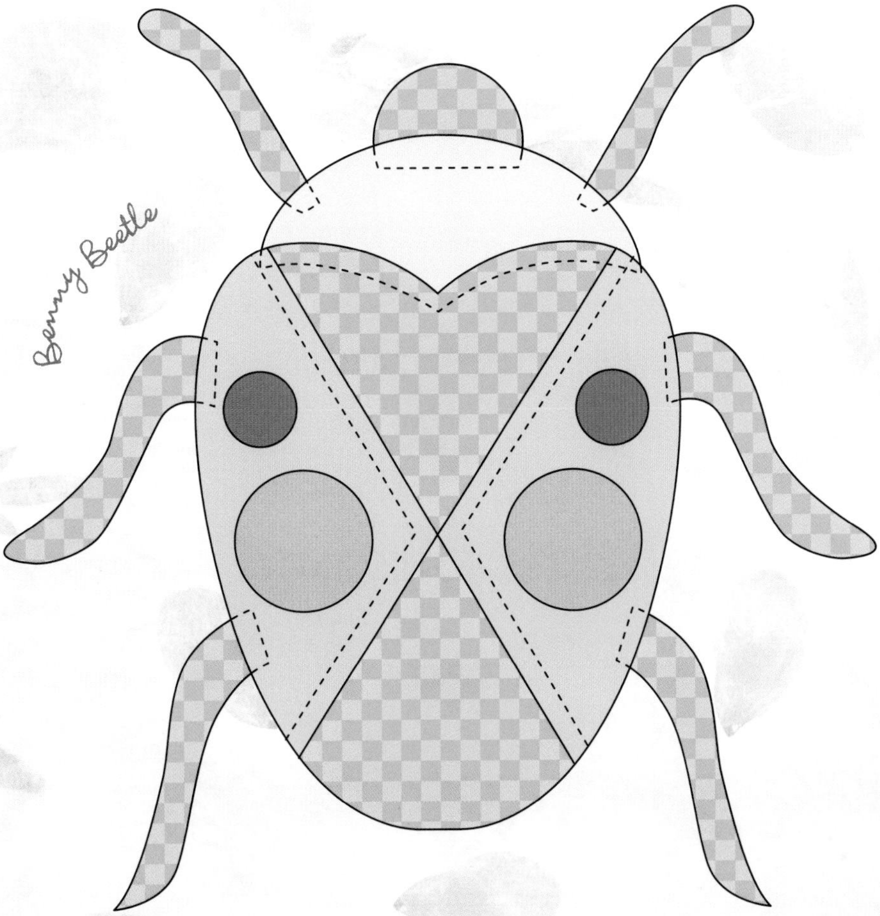

Benny Beetle

Tracing Line _____

Tracing Line _ _ _ _ _ _ _ _ _ _ _ _
(will be hidden behind other fabrics)

Embroidery Line _____

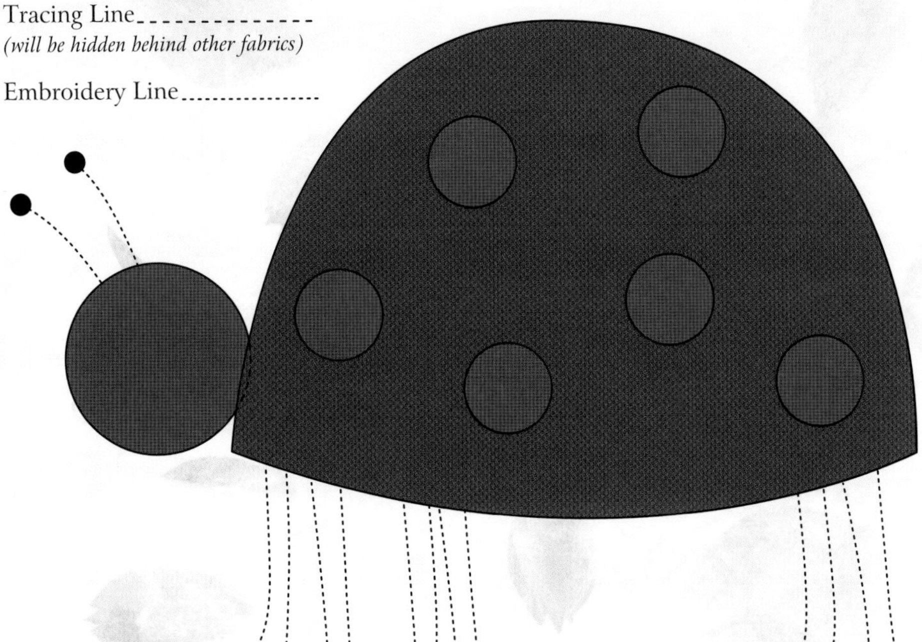

LuLu Ladybug

Bug Love Bed Quilt
Quick-Fuse Pattern

*Appliqué pattern is reversed for use with
Quick-Fuse Appliqué
(page 109)*

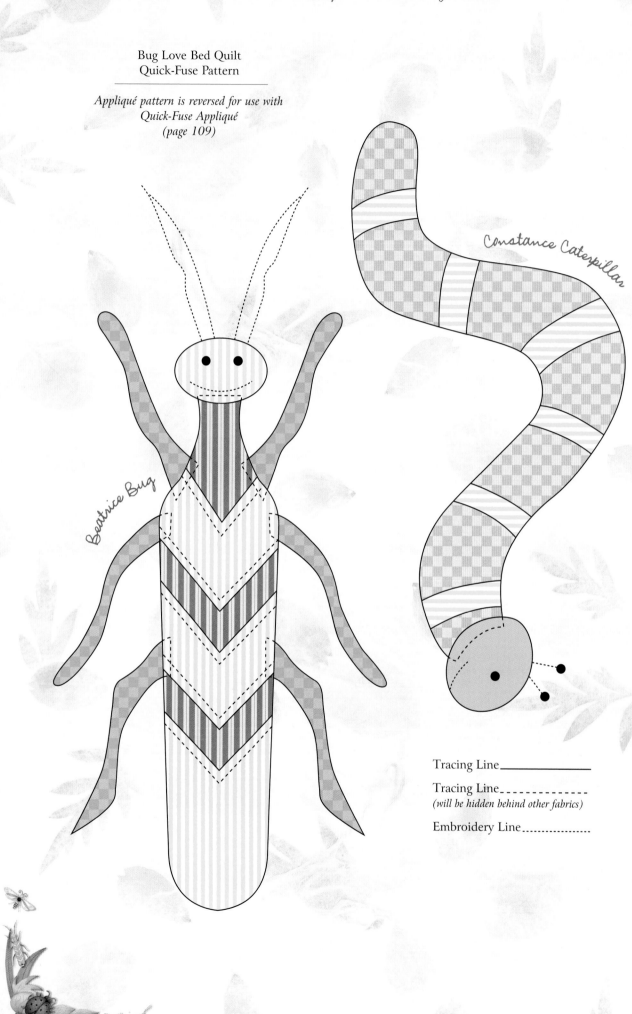

Constance Caterpillar

Beatrice Bug

Tracing Line————————

Tracing Line - - - - - - - - - -
(will be hidden behind other fabrics)

Embroidery Line ....

Adding the Appliqués

The instructions given are for the Quick-Fuse Appliqué method. If you prefer traditional hand appliqué, be sure to reverse all appliqué templates and add 1/4" seam allowances when cutting appliqué pieces. Refer to Hand Appliqué on page 109.

1. Cut four 5" squares from Cornerstone Fabric.

2. Refer to Quick-Fuse Appliqué directions on page 109. Trace patterns and use assorted scraps to make butterflies and dragonflies. Referring to photo for placement, arrange and fuse appliqués for each butterfly or dragonfly on 5" square. Finish edges with machine satin stitch or decorative stitching as desired. Embroider bug antennae. Square Cornerstones to 4 1/2" square. These appliqué Cornerstone squares will be used in Quilt Assembly on page 105.

Garden Glories Quilt photo page 10.

Enlarge butterflies and dragonflies 150% for Bug Love Quilt

Tracing Line ——————

Tracing Line - - - - - - - -
(will be hidden behind other fabrics)

Embroidery Line · · · · · · · · ·

August 24

My little patch of lavender is just about ready to harvest. The sweet scent fills the air reminding me that I need to make sachets and dry some of this fragrant herb for scones later this winter.

Lavender Plant in Bloom

Touch of yellow

Checklist

- ☑ Order seeds and bulbs for fall planting
- ☐ Harvest lavender
- ☐ Prune rambler roses

Coneflower Blossom

Lavender
~ Calming, relaxing
~ Great seasoning
~ Soothes the tummy
~ Aids sleep

Refreshing Lavender

Prairie House Lavender Farm

marker

Passed a whole field of lavender at a nearby farm. Waves of purple and green stretched across the field making a cloud of calming color.

LAVENDER FIELDS

77" × 91" BED QUILT AND PILLOW

A cloud of calming color can be yours every day when you make this prettily pieced bed quilt. The coordinating pillow features a pocket that can be filled with lavender so that you'll sleep the night away surrounded by beauty and soothing scents.

FABRIC REQUIREMENTS AND CUTTING INSTRUCTIONS

Read all instructions before beginning and use 1/4"-wide seam allowances throughout. Read Cutting the Strips and Pieces on page 108 prior to cutting fabrics.

Lavender Fields Bed Quilt 77" x 91"	FIRST CUT		SECOND CUT	
	Number of Strips or Pieces	Dimensions	Number of Pieces	Dimensions
Fabric A Background 1 1/8 yards	15	2 1/2" x 42"	240	2 1/2" squares
Fabric B Field Accent 1 1/2 yards	20	2 1/2" x 42"	320	2 1/2" squares
Fabric C Lavender Field 1 7/8 yards	25	2 1/2" x 42"	160 80	2 1/2" x 4 1/2" 2 1/2" squares
Fabric D Accent Squares 5/8 yard	7	2 1/2" x 42"	100	2 1/2" squares
Fabric E Lattice 1 1/8 yards	14	2 1/2" x 42"	80	2 1/2" x 6 1/2"
BORDERS				
First Border 1/3 yard	7	1 1/4" x 42"		
Outside Border 5 yards or 2 1/2 yards for non-directional fabric	2 2	9 3/4" x 96" 9 3/4" x 82"		
Binding 3/4 yard	9	2 3/4" x 42"		
Batting - 83" x 97" Backing - 5 1/2 yards				

MAKING THE BLOCKS

You will be making twenty Lavender Fields Blocks. Blocks measure 14 1/2" unfinished. Whenever possible, use the Assembly Line Method on page 108. Press seams in direction of arrows.

LAVENDER FIELDS BLOCKS

1. Refer to Quick Corner Triangles on page 108. Sew 2 1/2" Fabric B square to 2 1/2" Fabric A square as shown. Press. Make one hundred sixty.

A = 2 1/2 x 2 1/2
B = 2 1/2 x 2 1/2
Make 160

2. Sew 2 1/2" Fabric A square to unit from step 1 as shown. Press. Make eighty.

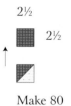

Make 80

3. Sew 2 1/2" Fabric C square to unit from step 1 as shown. Press. Make eighty.

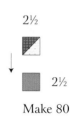

Make 80

4. Sew units from steps 2 and 3 together as shown. Press. Make eighty.

Make 80

5. Making a quick corner triangle unit, sew 2 1/2" Fabric B square to 2 1/2" x 4 1/2" Fabric C piece as shown. Press. Make eighty.

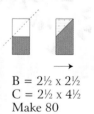

B = 2 1/2 x 2 1/2
C = 2 1/2 x 4 1/2
Make 80

6. Sew unit from step 5 to unit from step 4 as shown. Press. Make eighty.

Make 80

Lavender Sprigs

7. Making a quick corner triangle unit, sew 2¹/2" Fabric B square to 2¹/2" x 4¹/2" Fabric C piece as shown. Press. Make eighty.

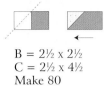

B = 2½ x 2½
C = 2½ x 4½
Make 80

8. Sew unit from step 7 to 2¹/2" Fabric D square as shown. Press. Make eighty.

2½

2½

Make 80

9. Sew unit from step 6 to unit from step 8 as shown. Press. Make eighty.

Make 80

10. Sew a 2¹/2" x 6¹/2" Fabric E piece between two units from step 9 as shown. Press. Make forty.

2½

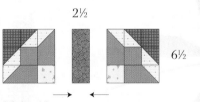

6½

Make 40

11. Sew a 2¹/2" Fabric D square between two 2¹/2" x 6¹/2" Fabric E pieces as shown. Press. Make twenty.

6½   2½   6½

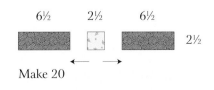

2½

Make 20

12. Sew unit from step 11 between two units from step 10 as shown. Press. Make twenty Lavender Fields Blocks. Block measures 14¹/2" square.

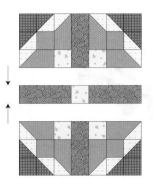

Make 20
Block measures
14½" square

ASSEMBLY

1. Refer to quilt layout below and photo on page 63. Arrange and sew blocks in five horizontal rows of four blocks each. Press seams in opposite directions from row to row.

2. Sew rows together. Press.

3. Sew 1¹/4" x 42" First Border strips end to end to make one continuous 1¹/4"-wide strip. Referring to Adding the Borders on page 110, measure quilt through center from side to side. Cut two 1¹/4"-wide First Border strips to that measurement. Sew to top and bottom of quilt. Press toward border.

Lavender Fields Bed Quilt
Finished Size: 77" x 91"; Photo: page 63

4. Measure quilt through center from top to bottom, including borders just added. Cut two 1¼"-wide First Border strips to that measurement. Sew to sides of quilt. Press toward border.

5. Refer to Mitered Borders on page 110. Sew two 9¾" x 82" Outside Border strips to top and bottom of quilt. Press toward border. Sew two 9¾" x 96" Outside Border strips to sides. Press. Miter corners. (*For non-directional fabric, cut nine 9¾" x 42" Outside Border strips. Sew 9¾" x 42" strips end to end to make one continuous 9¾"-wide strip. Refer to Adding the Borders on page 110 to add borders*).

LAYERING AND FINISHING

1. Cut backing in half crosswise. Sew pieces together to make one 83½" x 99" (approximate) piece. Press. Arrange and baste backing, batting, and top together, referring to Layering the Quilt on page 110.

2. Hand or machine quilt as desired.

3. Sew the 2¾" x 42" binding strips end to end to make one 2¾"-wide continuous strip. Referring to Binding the Quilt on page 111 and bind quilt to finish.

Prairie House Lavender
8205 N. Five Mile Road
Spokane, WA 99208
(509) 464-1449
mcswish@msn.com

Lavender Fields Pillow

Lavender Fields Pillow 18" square		
FIRST CUT		
	Number of Strips or Pieces	Dimensions
Fabric A Background, Pocket Trim, and Outside Border ½ yard	1	8½" square
	1	4½" x 5½"
	2	3" x 18½"
	2	3" x 13½"
Fabric B Triangles and Pocket ¼ yard	1*	8" square
	8	2½" squares
Fabric C Block Corners ¼ yard	4	2½" x 6½"
	4	2½" x 4½"
First Border ⅛ yard	2	1" x 13½"
	2	1" x 12½"
Backing ⅜ yard	2	12" x 18½"
Lining - 22" square Batting - 22" square Pillow Form - 13" *For non-embroidered pocket, cut one 4½" x 4" piece*		

MAKING THE PILLOW

For our pocket, we scanned the coneflower on page 67 and digitized the flower for an embroidery unit. The flower was embroidered on an 8" Fabric B square and trimmed to 4½" x 4". You may choose to appliqué or hand embroider the flower.

1. Refer to Quick Corner Triangles on page 108. Sew 2½" Fabric B square to 2½" x 4½" Fabric C piece as shown. Press. Make four, two of each variation.

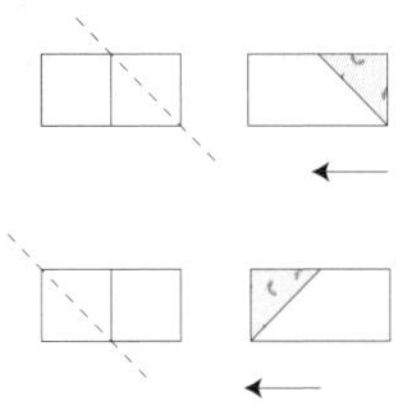

B = 2½ x 2½
C = 2½ x 4½
Make 4
(2 of each variation)

2. Sew two units from step 1 together as shown. Press. Make two.

Make 2

3. Sew 8½" Fabric A square between units from step 2. Press.

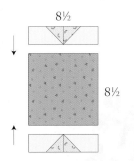

4. Making quick corner triangle units, sew 2½" Fabric B square to 2½" x 6½" Fabric C piece as shown. Press. Make four, two of each variation.

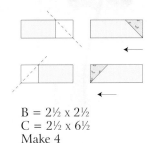

B = 2½ x 2½
C = 2½ x 6½
Make 4
(2 of each variation)

5. Sew two units from step 4 together as shown. Press. Make two.

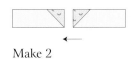

Make 2

6. Sew unit from step 3 between units from step 5 as shown. Press.

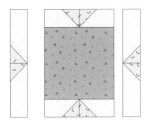

7. Referring to pillow layout and photo, sew unit from step 6 between two 1" x 12½" First Border strips. Press seams toward border. Sew this unit between two 1" x 13½" First Border strips. Press.

8. Sew unit from step 7 between two 3" x 13½" Outside Border strips. Press seams toward Outside Border. Sew this unit between two 3" x 18½" Outside Border strips. Press.

9. Refer to Finishing Pillows on page 111, step 1, to quilt pillow top.

10. Sew 4½" x 5½" Fabric A piece to embroidered 4½" x 4" Fabric B piece as shown. Press.

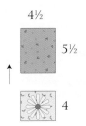

11. Fold unit from step 10 in half crosswise, right sides together, and stitch raw edges together using a ¼"-wide seam allowance and leaving a 2½" opening for turning as shown. Clip corners, turn right side out, and press. Hand stitch opening closed.

12. Referring to layout below, position and sew pocket from step 11 to center of pillow top.

13. Refer to Finishing Pillows on page 111 to sew backing to pillow and make pillow form, if desired. Stitch between Outside Border and First Border through all layers to create a flange. Insert 13" pillow form in pillow and a small bouquet of lavender in pocket if desired.

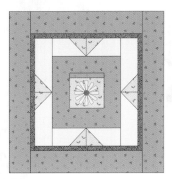

Coneflower Embroidery Template

August Block of the Month Day Lily (Bottom Left) Garden Glories Quilt photo page 10		
	FIRST CUT	
	Number of Strips or Pieces	Dimensions
Fabric A Background 1/4 yard	1	4 1/2" square
	1	4" square
	1	3 1/2" square
	1	2 1/2" x 3 1/2"
	4	2 1/2" squares
	2	1 1/2" x 5 1/2"
	2	1 1/2" x 4"
	2	1 1/2" x 2"
	17	1 1/2" squares
Fabric B Dark Petals 1/8 yard	2	2 1/2" squares
	2	1 1/2" x 3 1/2"
Fabric C Light Petals Scrap	1	3 1/2" x 5 1/2"
	1	3 1/2" x 2 1/2"
Fabric D Petal Tip Scrap	2	1 1/2" squares
Fabric E Dark Leaf 1/8 yard - total of two fabrics	1	2 1/2" x 3 1/2"
	1	2" x 5 1/2"
	1	2" x 4"
	2	2" x 2 1/2"
	5	1 1/2" squares
Fabric F Light Leaf Scrap	2	1 1/2" x 5 1/2"

Three 5/8" oval beads
Embroidery floss

Assembly

1. Referring to Quick Corner Triangles on page 108, sew 2 1/2" Fabric A square to 2 1/2" Fabric B square as shown. Press. Sew 1 1/2" Fabric A square to this unit as shown. Press. Make two.

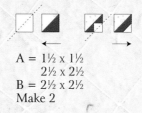

A = 1 1/2 x 1 1/2
    2 1/2 x 2 1/2
B = 2 1/2 x 2 1/2
Make 2

2. Making a quick corner triangle unit, sew 1 1/2" Fabric A square to 1 1/2" Fabric D square. Press. Make two. Sew 1 1/2" Fabric A square to each unit as shown. Press. Make one of each variation.

A = 1 1/2 x 1 1/2
D = 1 1/2 x 1 1/2
Make 2

1 1/2   1 1/2

          1 1/2

Make 1 of each variation

3. Making a quick corner triangle unit, sew 1 1/2" Fabric E square to 2 1/2" x 3 1/2" Fabric A piece as shown. Press.

E = 1 1/2 x 1 1/2
A = 2 1/2 x 3 1/2

4. Making a quick corner triangle unit, sew 1 1/2" Fabric A square to 1 1/2" x 3 1/2" Fabric B piece as shown. Press. Make one of each variation.

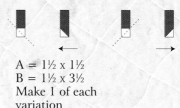

A = 1 1/2 x 1 1/2
B = 1 1/2 x 3 1/2
Make 1 of each variation

5. Sew units from steps 1, 2, and 3 together as shown. Press. Sew unit from step 4 to 3 1/2" x 5 1/2" Fabric C piece as shown. Press. Sew units together. Press.

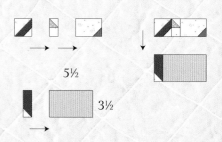

5 1/2

3 1/2

6. Making quick corner triangle units, sew 1 1/2" Fabric A and 2 1/2" Fabric A squares to 2 1/2" x 3 1/2" Fabric E piece as shown. Press. Sew unit to 2 1/2" Fabric A square. Press.

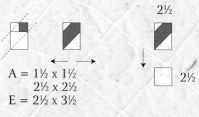

A = 1 1/2 x 1 1/2
    2 1/2 x 2 1/2
E = 2 1/2 x 3 1/2

2 1/2

2 1/2

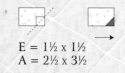

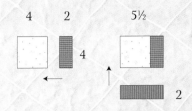

7. Sew units from steps 5 and 6 together as shown. Press.

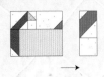

8. Sew remaining unit from step 4 to 3½" x 2½" Fabric C piece as shown. Press. Sew remaining units from steps 1 and 2 together. Press. Arrange and sew these units and 3½" Fabric A square together as shown. Press.

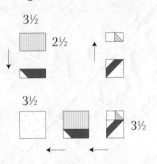

9. Sew units from steps 7 and 8 together as shown. Press. Block measures 8½" square.

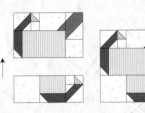

Block measures
8½" square

10. Making quick corner triangle units, sew two 1½" Fabric A squares to 1½" x 5½" Fabric F piece as shown. Press. Sew unit to 1½" x 5½" Fabric A piece. Press. Make two.

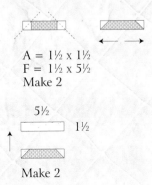

A = 1½ x 1½
F = 1½ x 5½
Make 2

5½ ☐ 1½

Make 2

11. Making a quick corner triangle unit, sew 1½" Fabric A square to 1½" Fabric E square as shown. Press. Make four. Sew 1½" x 2" Fabric A piece between quick corner triangle units as shown. Press. Make two, one of each variation.

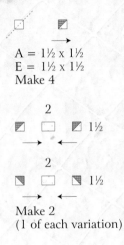

A = 1½ x 1½
E = 1½ x 1½
Make 4

2
☑ ☐ ☑ 1½

2
◩ ☐ ◩ 1½

Make 2
(1 of each variation)

12. Sew unit from step 11 to 1½" x 4" Fabric A piece as shown. Press. Make two, one of each variation. Sew these units to 2" x 2½" Fabric E pieces as shown. Press. Make one of each variation.

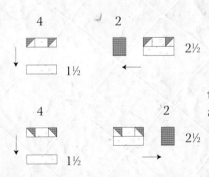

4   2
◩ ☐   ☐ ◩ 2½
☐ 1½

4   2
◩ ☐   ☐ ◩ 2½
☐ 1½

13. Sew unit from step 10 to unit from step 12 as shown. Press. Make one of each variation.

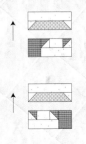

14. Sew 4" Fabric A square to 2" x 4" Fabric E piece. Press. Sew unit to 2" x 5½" Fabric E piece as shown. Press.

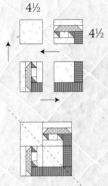

4   2   5½
        4
                2

15. Sew together 4½" Fabric A square and units from step 13 and step 14 as shown. Press. Draw a diagonal line on the unit as shown. Stitch ⅛" from each side of the drawn line. Carefully cut the unit on the drawn line to make two leaf units.

4½
    4½

Block measures
9½" square

16. Sew a leaf unit from step 15 to two sides of the Day Lily block as shown. Press.

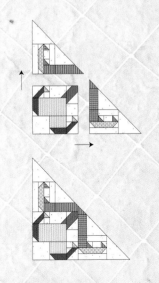

September 4

The pear tree in the backyard is filled with gorgeous golden pears. We're really enjoying the delicious taste of these juicy beauties. Grapes are dripping from the arbor ... so pretty that we packed a picnic and had lunch there. These late summer days are fleeting ~ we will enjoy them while we can!

Ready for picking

Crimson Cuties

Checklist

- ☑ Pick fruit
- ☐ Plant evergreen hedges
- ☑ Pick flowers to dry and press
- ☐ Harvest herbs

Coral Bells

Grapes fit for a King!

Perfect Pear

Berry Bunch

Reread Keat's Ode to Autumn ~
Thought this was particularly appropriate!

"Season of mists and mellow fruitfulness,
Close bosom friend of the maturing sun;
Conspiring with him how to load and bless
With fruit the vines that round the
thatch-eaves run."

PEAR PERFECTION

35" x 32³/4" WALL QUILT

Harvest a crop of pleasure every time you look at this beautiful wall quilt or use the matching tablecloth. Trapunto quilting adds dimension to the pears while an easy Seminole Patchwork technique makes short work of the checked tiles.

FABRIC REQUIREMENTS AND CUTTING INSTRUCTIONS

Read all instructions before beginning and use 1/4"-wide seam allowances throughout. Read Cutting the Strips and Pieces on page 108 prior to cutting fabrics.

Pear Perfection Wall Quilt 35" x 32³/4"		
	FIRST CUT	
	Number of Strips or Pieces	Dimensions
Fabric A Background 1/2 yard	1	16¹/2" x 26¹/2"
Fabric B Tile Accent 1/8 yard	1	1" x 26¹/2"
Fabric C Second Tile Accent 1/8 yard	1	2" x 26¹/2"
Fabric D Dark Patchwork Tile 1/4 yard	3	2¹/2" x 42"
Fabric E Light Patchwork Tile 1/4 yard	2	2¹/2" x 42"
Fabric F Bowl and Rim *assorted fabrics to total* 7/8 yard	4 2	4¹/2" x 42" 3¹/2" x 42"
Fabric G 1/3 yard	2	8¹/2" squares
BORDERS		
First Border 1/4 yard	4	1¹/2" x 42"
Outside Border 1/2 yard	4	3¹/2" x 42"
Binding 3/8 yard	4	2³/4" x 42"
Appliqué Pears, Leaves, and Stems - assorted scraps to total 1/3 yard Backing - 1 yard Batting - 38¹/2" x 36" lightweight and 4" x 17" high loft Lightweight Fusible Web - 3/4 yard Oil Pastels - optional Temporary Spray Adhesive		

MAKING THE QUILT

This quilt consists of several techniques: Seminole Patchwork piecing, fabric weaving, appliqué, dimensional appliqué, and trapunto. Whenever possible, use the Assembly Line Method on page 108. Refer to Accurate Seam Allowance on page 108 prior to making quilt. Press in the direction of arrows.

CENTER PANEL ASSEMBLY

1. Sew 1" x 26¹/2" Fabric B strip between 16¹/2" x 26¹/2" Fabric A piece and 2" x 26¹/2" Fabric C strip as shown. Press.

2. Sew three alternating 2¹/2" x 42" Fabric D strips and two 2¹/2" x 42" Fabric E strips together as shown. Press toward Fabric D. Cut twelve 2¹/2"-wide segments.

Cut 12 segments

3. Sew segments from step 2 together in pairs as shown to create tile pattern. Press. Sew pairs together to make one unit as shown. Press. Cut 26¹/2" x 6¹/4" rectangle as shown. Rectangle will extend 1/4" past the tile points allowing for seam allowances.

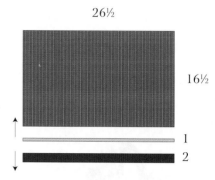

4. Sew rectangle unit from step 3 to unit from step 1 as shown. Press.

ADDING THE BORDERS

1. Referring to Adding the Borders on page 110, measure quilt through center from side to side. Cut two 1¹/₂"-wide First Border strips to that measurement. Sew to top and bottom of quilt. Press toward border.

2. Measure quilt through center from top to bottom, including borders just added. Cut two 1¹/₂"-wide First Border strips to that measurement. Sew to sides of quilt. Press toward border.

3. Repeat steps 1 and 2 to sew the 3¹/₂"-wide Outside Border strips to top, bottom, and sides of quilt. Press toward border.

MAKING THE BOWL

1. Fold one 4¹/₂" x 42" Fabric F strip lengthwise with right sides together. Sew along length of strip. Turn the tube of fabric right side out. Center seam on back and press. Repeat process with remaining 4¹/₂"-wide Fabric F strips. Cut fabric tubes into three 18" lengths and six 10" lengths.

42

Seam → allowance

2. Using one 3¹/₂" x 42" Fabric F strip, make a tube as in step 1. (Remaining 3¹/₂" strip will be used later for the rim). Cut fabric tube into one 18" length and two 10" lengths.

Miniature Strawberries

Pear Perfection Wall Quilt
Finished Size: 35" x 32³/4"; Photo: page 71

3. Refer to Quick-Fuse Appliqué on page 109. Trace one Bowl Template on page 76 onto fusible web. Cut out bowl 1/4" beyond traced line. Place on a flat, heat-resistant surface with fusible side up. Referring to photos on page 71 and at right, arrange eight 10" fabric tubes from steps 1 and 2 side by side vertically over fusible web. Pin in place at top. Weave 18" fabric tubes horizontally in an over-one, under-one pattern until all areas of fusible web are covered.

Pear Perfection Tablecloth

Finished Size: 52" x 52"

sixteen 2¹/2"-wide segments from step 2 together. Press. Make two. Cut into 38" x 6¹/4" rectangle. Edges will extend 1/4" past the tile points allowing for seam allowances. Sew to opposite sides of unit from step 1.

4. Sew twenty 2¹/2"-wide segments from step 2 together. Press. Make two. Cut into two 49¹/2" x 6¹/4" rectangles. Sew to remaining sides. Press.

5. Sew 3¹/2" x 42" Fabric C strips end to end to make one continuous 3¹/2"-wide strip. Press. Measure quilt through center from side to side. Trim two 3¹/2"-wide strips to that measurement. Sew to opposite sides of quilt. Press.

6. Measure quilt through center from top to bottom, including borders just added. Trim two 3¹/2"-wide Fabric C strips to this measurement. Sew to sides. Press.

7. Press under 1/4" along outside edge. Fold Outside Border in half lengthwise, wrong sides together. Press and pin in place. Hand stitch to finish.

Fabric Requirements

Fabric A Center Panel - (1¹/8 yards)
One 36¹/2" square

Fabric B Accent Trim - (1/4 yard)
Two 1¹/4" x 36¹/2" strips
Two 1¹/4" x 38" strips

Fabric C Outside Border - (2/3 yard)
Six 3¹/2" x 42" strips

Fabric D Dark Patchwork Tile
(1¹/8 yards)
Fifteen 2¹/2" x 42" strips

Fabric E Light Patchwork Tile
(3/4 yard)
Ten 2¹/2" x 42" strips

Making the Table Cloth

1. Sew 36¹/2" Fabric A square between two 1¹/4" x 36¹/2" Fabric B strips. Press. Sew this unit between two 1¹/4" x 38" Fabric B strips. Press.

2. Referring to Pear Perfection Wall Quilt step 2 on page 72, sew Fabric D and E strips together to make five strip sets. Cut seventy-two 2¹/2"-wide segments.

3. Referring to Pear Perfection Wall Quilt step 3 on page 72, sew

4. Press fusible web to bowl unit according to the manufacturer's directions.

5. After piece has cooled, cut bowl on traced lines. Referring to quilt layout on page 73 and photo on page 71, arrange and fuse bowl to center panel, finish with machine satin stitch or decorative stitching as desired.

6. Make Bowl Rim Pattern and cut two rims from remaining 3¹/2" x 42" Fabric F strip. Place fabric pieces, right sides together, on top of 4" x 17" batting. Sew the three layers together, leaving a 4" opening for turning as shown. Trim and clip curves. Turn bowl rim right side out. Press. Hand stitch seam opening closed.

4" opening

7. Mark Leaf Quilting Template on bowl rim. Hand or machine quilt as desired.

8. Sew two 8¹/2" Fabric G squares right sides together, leaving a 4" opening for turning. Clip corners and turn napkin square right side out. Press. Hand stitch opening closed. Topstitch ¹/8" from edges of napkin. Press.

9. Referring to quilt layout on page 73 and photo on page 71, arrange napkin on rim. Fold excess fabric behind rim and tack in place. Set rim aside for now.

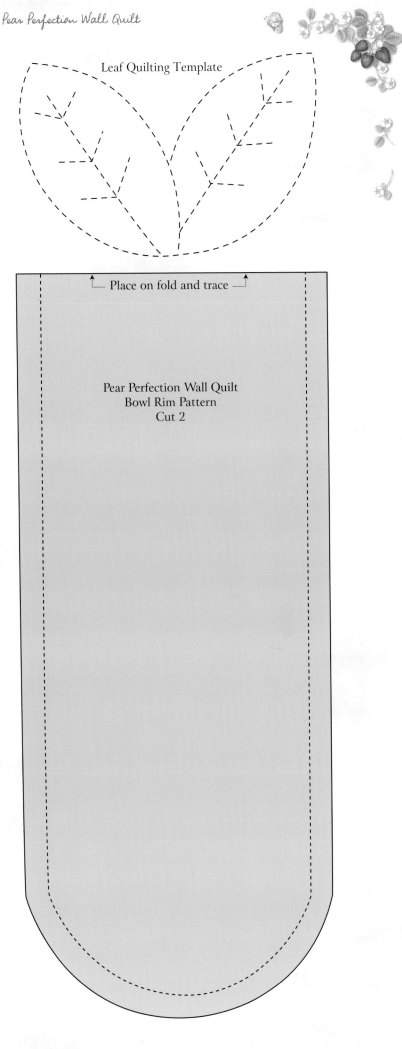

Leaf Quilting Template

Place on fold and trace

Pear Perfection Wall Quilt
Bowl Rim Pattern
Cut 2

APPLIQUÉING THE C ENTER PANEL

The instructions given are for Quick-Fuse Appliqué method. If you prefer hand appliqué, be sure to reverse all appliqué templates and add ¼" seam allowances when cutting appliqué pieces. Refer to Hand Appliqué directions on page 109.

1. Refer to Quick-Fuse Appliqué on page 109. Trace appliqué patterns on page 77 for pear, stem, and leaf. Use assorted scraps to trace and cut five pears, five stems, and seven leaves.

2. Referring to quilt layout on page 73, arrange and fuse appliqués in place and finish with decorative stitching as desired.

3. Referring to quilt photo on page 71, position quilted bowl rim and napkin over top of bowl and bottom of pears. Hand stitch sides and lower section of bowl rim to center panel.

⌐ Place on folded paper and trace ⌐

Pear Perfection Wall Quilt
Bowl Pattern

Shading Pears

To give your pears the look of real fruit, shade them with high quality oil pastels. Rub your finger on the color and with a soft touch lightly apply color to the side of each pear to add depth and shading. Place piece of paper over the pears and heat-set the pastel shading for a few seconds with a dry iron on cotton setting to make color permanent.

LAYERING AND BINDING

1. Using tracing paper, trace an outline of your pear arrangement. Use this pattern to cut the shape from a 4" x 17" piece of high-loft batting. Using temporary spray adhesive, place batting on wrong side of quilt behind pears.

2. Cut backing and lightweight batting to 38½" x 36". Arrange and baste backing, batting, and top together, referring to Layering the Quilt on page 110.

3. Hand or machine quilt as desired. Hint: Heavier quilting will be needed on the background to give pears a trapunto effect.

4. Sew 2¾" x 42" binding strips end to end to make one continuous 2¾"-wide binding strip. Press. Refer to Binding the Quilt on page 111 and bind quilt to finish.

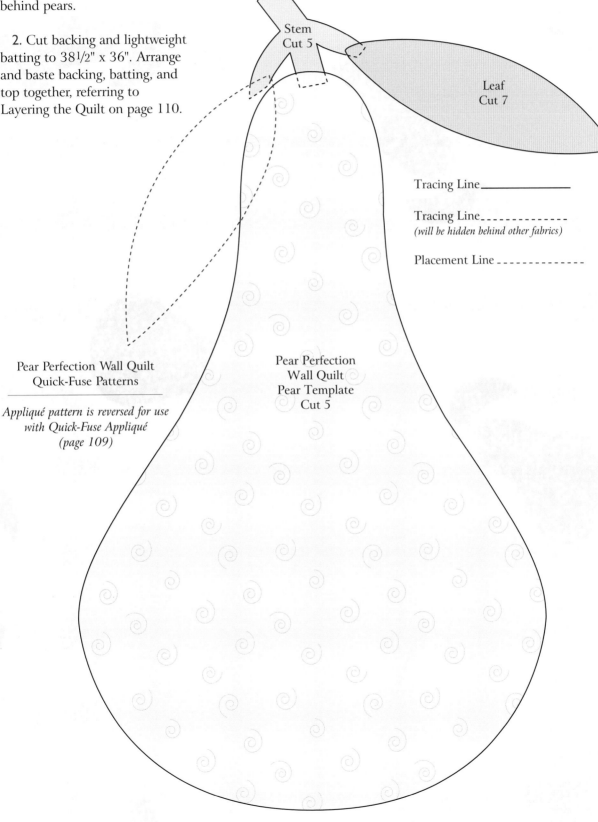

Stem
Cut 5

Leaf
Cut 7

Tracing Line _____

Tracing Line - - - - - - - - - - -
(will be hidden behind other fabrics)

Placement Line - - - - - - - - - - -

Pear Perfection Wall Quilt
Quick-Fuse Patterns

*Appliqué pattern is reversed for use
with Quick-Fuse Appliqué
(page 109)*

Pear Perfection
Wall Quilt
Pear Template
Cut 5

September
FRITILLARY
BLOCK OF THE MONTH

September Block of the Month Fritillary (Top Left) Garden Glories Quilt photo page 10		
	FIRST CUT	
	Number of Strips or Pieces	Dimensions
Fabric A Background ¼ yard	1	5" square
	1	2½" x 6"
	1	2½" x 4"
	2	2½" squares
	1	2" x 9½"
	1	2" x 8"
	2	2" squares
	4	1½" x 2½"
	12	1½" squares
	1	1" x 4½"
	1	1" x 4"
Fabric B Flower Center Scrap	1	4" square
Fabric C Light Flower Petal ¼ yard* (⅛ yard for non-directional fabric)	1	6½" x 2½"
	1	4½" x 2½"
	1	2½" square
Fabric D Medium Flower Petal ¼ yard* (⅛ yard for non-directional fabric)	1	6½" x 2½"
	1	4½" x 2½"
	1	2½" square
		* For directional fabric the measurement listed first runs parallel to selvage (strip width).

September Block of the Month Fritillary Continued		
	FIRST CUT	
	Number of Strips or Pieces	Dimensions
Fabric E Dark Flower Petal Scrap	2	1½" x 2½"
Fabric F Dark Leaf Scrap	1	1½" x 6"
	1	1½" x 5"
Fabric G Light Leaf Scrap	2	1½" x 2½"

Assembly

1. Referring to Quick Corner Triangles on page 108, sew two 2" Fabric A squares to opposite corners of 4" Fabric B square as shown. Press.

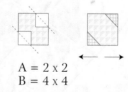

A = 2 x 2
B = 4 x 4

2. Sew 1" x 4" Fabric A piece to unit from step 1 as shown. Press. Sew unit to 1" x 4½" Fabric A piece as shown. Press.

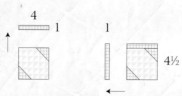

3. Making quick corner triangle units, sew 2½" Fabric A square to 4½" x 2½" Fabric C piece as shown. Press. Sew 2½" Fabric A and 2½" Fabric C squares to 6½" x 2½" Fabric C piece as shown. Press.

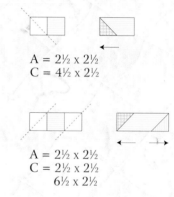

A = 2½ x 2½
C = 4½ x 2½

A = 2½ x 2½
C = 2½ x 2½
6½ x 2½

Note: If you are using striped fabric for Fabric C, you may want to cut 2½" Fabric C square carefully so the stripes align when joined to 6½" x 2½" Fabric C piece.

4. Sew first unit from step 3 to unit from step 2 as shown. Press. Sew this unit to remaining unit from step 3 as shown. Press.

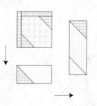

5. Making quick corner triangle units, sew two 1½" Fabric A squares to 1½" × 2½" Fabric E piece as shown. Press. Make two, one of each variation.

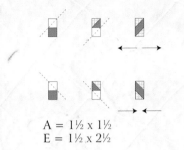

A = 1½ x 1½
E = 1½ x 2½

6. Making quick corner triangle units, sew 1½" Fabric A square to 4½" × 2½" Fabric D piece as shown. Press. Sew 1½" Fabric A and 2½" Fabric D squares to 6½" × 2½" Fabric D piece as shown. Press.

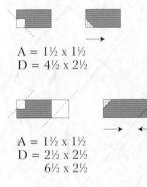

A = 1½ x 1½
D = 4½ x 2½

A = 1½ x 1½
D = 2½ x 2½
     6½ x 2½

Note: If you are using striped fabric for Fabric D, you may want to cut 2½" Fabric D square carefully so the stripes align when joined to 6½" × 2½" Fabric D piece.

7. Sew first unit from step 5 between 1½" × 2½" Fabric A piece and first unit from step 6 as shown. Press. Sew remaining unit from step 5 between 1½" × 2½" Fabric A piece and remaining unit from step 6 as shown. Press.

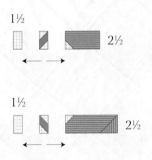

1½

2½

1½

2½

8. Sew unit from step 4 and units from step 7 together as shown. Press. Block measures 8½" square.

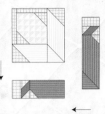

Block measures
8½" square

9. Making quick corner triangle units, sew two 1½" Fabric A squares to 1½" × 2½" Fabric G piece as shown. Press. Make two.

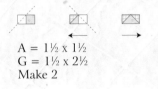

A = 1½ x 1½
G = 1½ x 2½
Make 2

10. Sew unit from step 9 between 2½" × 4" and 1½" × 2½" Fabric A pieces as shown. Press. Sew remaining unit from step 9 between 2½" × 6" and 1½" × 2½" Fabric A pieces as shown. Press.

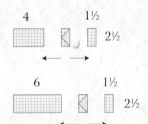

4   1½

          2½

6   1½

          2½

11. Making quick corner triangle units, sew 1½" Fabric A square to 1½" × 5" Fabric F piece as shown. Press. Sew 1½" Fabric A square to 1½" × 6" Fabric F piece as shown. Press.

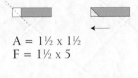

A = 1½ x 1½
F = 1½ x 5

A = 1½ x 1½
F = 1½ x 6

12. Sew units from step 11 to sides of 5" Fabric A square as shown. Press.

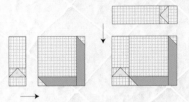

5

    5

13. Sew units from step 10 to unit from step 12 as shown. Press.

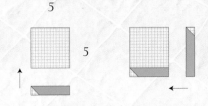

14. Sew unit from step 13 to 2" × 8" Fabric A piece. Press. Sew this unit to 2" × 9½" Fabric A piece. Press. Block measures 9½" square. Draw a diagonal line on the unit as shown. Stitch ⅛" from each side of the drawn line. Carefully cut the unit on the drawn line to make two leaf units.

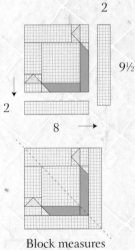

2

9½

2

8

Block measures
9½" square

15. Sew leaf unit from step 14 to two sides of the Fritillary Block as shown. Press.

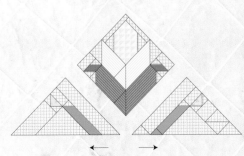

The colors of Autumn

I've started collecting acorns and buckeyes to use in my fall decorating. Each day I pick up a few perfect leaves and press them within the pages of my telephone book. In a week or two, I'll pull them out, nicely preserved, to grace my tabletop.

early acorn

Ninebark leaf

Colors of an autumn rainbow

festive fall stamp

OCTOBER

14 CENTS

October 10

The days are getting shorter ... long shadows already cross the lawn. The dark greens of lawn and shadows are surprised into wakefulness by the glorious profusion of color in the treetops! Already the boldly colored leaves are beginning to drift to the ground.

Preserving Leaves~

Cover with glycerin/ water mix
Iron leaves with waxed paper
Stick in phone book!

Leafy green display

acorn

filbert

Fresh fallen nuts

Changing colors!

Gold and burgundy mums provide mounds of color in the garden. The ornamental cabbage looks great in the basket on the porch.

BLOWING IN THE WIND

77" x 97" BED QUILT

Colorful leaves drift to the ground on this warm and wonderful bed-size quilt. Leaves are randomly interspersed with solid color blocks making construction so easy, you'll have plenty of time to piece the border!

FABRIC REQUIREMENTS AND CUTTING INSTRUCTIONS

Read all instructions before beginning and use 1/4"-wide seam allowances throughout. Read Cutting the Strips and Pieces on page 108 prior to cutting fabrics.

Blowing In The Wind Bed Quilt 77" x 97"	FIRST CUT		SECOND CUT	
	Number of Strips or Pieces	Dimensions	Number of Pieces	Dimensions
Fabric A Block & Border Background 2 5/8 yards	8	2 1/2" x 42"	48	2 1/2" x 3 1/2"
			52	2 1/2" squares
	6	2" x 42"	120	2" squares
	35	1 1/2" x 42"	24	1 1/2" x 9 1/2"
			24	1 1/2" x 8 1/2"
			4	1 1/2" x 7 1/2"
			4	1 1/2" x 6 1/2"
			24	1 1/2" x 5 1/2"
			24	1 1/2" x 4 1/2"
			168	1 1/2" squares
Fabric B Light Leaf for Blocks & Border 3/8 yard for each of eight fabrics	1*	5" x 42"	2*	5" squares
	1*	2 1/2" x 42"	3*	2 1/2" x 5 1/2"
	cut for each fabric		3*	2 1/2" x 4 1/2"
	36**	3" x 6 1/2" (border)		
Fabric C Dark Leaf for Blocks & Border 3/8 yard for each of eight fabrics	1*	5" x 42"	2*	5" squares
	1*	2 1/2" x 42"	3*	2 1/2" x 7 1/2"
	cut for each fabric		3*	2 1/2" x 6 1/2"
	36**	3" x 6 1/2" (border)		
Fabric D Leaf Stem 1/6 yard	3	1 1/2" x 42"	24	1 1/2" x 2 1/2"
			24	1 1/2" squares
Fabric E Solid Blocks, Pieced Border & Corners 2/3 yard for each of six fabrics (variety of lights and darks)	24	10 1/2" squares		
	4	7" squares (corners)		
	40**	3" x 6 1/2" (border)		
BORDERS				
Accent Border 1/2 yard	9	1 1/2" x 42"	4	1 1/2" x 7 1/2"
Binding 7/8 yard	9	2 3/4" x 42"		

Backing - 7 1/4 yards
Batting - 85" x 105"
** Cut border pieces from remaining yardage.

MAKING THE BLOCKS

You will be making twenty-four Leaf Blocks and twenty-four plain blocks. All Leaf Blocks measure 10 1/2" square unfinished. Whenever possible, use the Assembly Line Method on page 108. Press seams in direction of arrows. Refer to Accurate Seam Allowance on page 108 prior to making quilt blocks.

LEAF BLOCKS

1. Draw a diagonal line on wrong side of 5" Fabric B square. Place one Fabric B square and one 5" Fabric C square right sides together. Sew a scant 1/4" away from drawn line on both sides to make half-square triangles as shown. Make two of each color combination for a total of sixteen. Cut on drawn line and press. This will make thirty-two half square triangles. Square to 4 1/2".

Fabric B = 5 x 5
Fabric C = 5 x 5
Make 16
(2 of each color combination)

Square to 4 1/2

2. Refer to Quick Corner Triangle directions on page 108. Sew a 2 1/2" Fabric A square to opposite corners of unit from step 1 as shown. Make sure all seams slant in same direction. Press. Make three of each color combination for a total of twenty-four.

A = 2 1/2 x 2 1/2
Make 24
(3 of each color combination)

Red Leaf

3. Sew 1¹/2" x 4¹/2" Fabric A strip to unit from step 2 as shown. Press. Sew 1¹/2" x 5¹/2" Fabric A strip to unit as shown. Press. Make three of each color combination for a total of twenty-four.

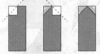

Make 24
(3 of each color combination)

4. Making quick corner triangle units, sew two 1¹/2" Fabric A squares to 2¹/2" x 5¹/2" Fabric B piece as shown. Press. Make three of each color combination for a total of twenty-four.

A = 1½ x 1½
B = 2½ x 5½
Make 24
(3 of each color combination)

5. Sew unit from step 3 to unit from step 4 as shown. Press. Make three of each color combination for a total of twenty-four.

Make 24
(3 of each color combination)

6. Making quick corner triangle units, sew two 1¹/2" Fabric A squares to 2¹/2" x 7¹/2" Fabric C piece as shown. Press. Make three of each color combination for a total of twenty-four.

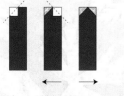

A = 1½ x 1½
C = 2½ x 7½
Make 24
(3 of each color combination)

7. Sew unit from step 6 to unit from step 5 as shown. Press. Make three of each color combination for a total of twenty-four.

Make 24
(3 of each color combination)

8. Making quick corner triangle units, sew 1¹/2" Fabric A square to 2¹/2" x 4¹/2" Fabric B piece as shown. Make three of each color combination for a total of twenty-four.

A = 1½ x 1½
B = 2½ x 4½
Make 24
(3 of each color combination)

Blowing in the Wind Bed Quilt
Finished Size: 77" x 97"; Photo: page 81

9. Sew 2¹/₂" x 3¹/₂" Fabric A piece to unit from step 8 as shown. Press. Make three of each color combination for a total of twenty-four.

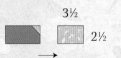

3½

2½

Make 24
(3 of each color combination)

10. Making quick corner triangle units, sew 1¹/₂" Fabric A square to 2¹/₂" x 6¹/₂" Fabric C piece as shown. Press. Make three of each color combination for a total of twenty-four.

A = 1½ x 1½
C = 2½ x 6½
Make 24
(3 of each color combination)

11. Sew 2¹/₂" x 3¹/₂" Fabric A piece to unit from step 10 as shown. Press. Make three of each color combination for a total of twenty-four.

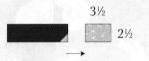

3½

2½

Make 24
(3 of each color combination)

12. Sew unit from step 9 to unit from step 7 as shown. Press. Sew unit from step 11 to same unit as shown. Press. Make three of each color combination for a total of twenty-four.

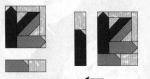

Make 24
(3 of each color combination)

13. Making quick corner triangle units, sew 1¹/₂" Fabric D square to 1¹/₂" x 9¹/₂" Fabric A piece as shown. Press. Make twenty-four.

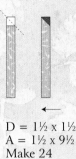

D = 1½ x 1½
A = 1½ x 9½
Make 24

14. Sew unit from step 13 to unit from step 12 as shown. Press. Make twenty-four.

Make 24

15. Making quick corner triangle units, sew 1¹/₂" Fabric A square to 1¹/₂" x 2¹/₂" Fabric D piece as shown. Press. Make twenty-four.

A = 1½ x 1½
D = 1½ x 2½
Make 24

16. Sew 1¹/₂" x 8¹/₂" Fabric A piece to unit from step 15 as shown. Press. Make twenty-four.

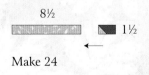

8½

1½

Make 24

17. Sew unit from step 16 to unit from step 14 as shown. Press. Make twenty-four Leaf Blocks.

Make 24
Block measures
10½" square

ASSEMBLY

1. Refer to quilt layout on page 83. Arrange and sew Leaf Blocks and 10¹/₂" Fabric E squares in eight horizontal rows of six blocks each. Press seams in opposite directions from row to row.

2. Sew rows together. Press. Measure quilt top to make sure it is 60¹/₂" x 80¹/₂".

MAKING THE BORDERS

The border consists of an Accent Border, fifty-six pieced leaves, and four Corner Leaves. Refer to Accurate Seam Allowance on page 108.

BORDER LEAF UNITS

1. Referring to photo on page 81 and quilt layout on page 83, sew 3" x 6¹/₂" Fabric B piece to 3" x 6¹/₂" Fabric C piece as shown. Press. Make thirty-six. Sew 3" x 6¹/₂" light Fabric E piece to 3" x 6¹/₂" dark Fabric E piece. Press. Make twenty.

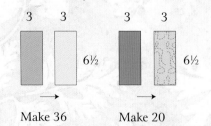

3   3   3   3

6½   6½

Make 36   Make 20

2. Making quick corner triangle units, sew two 2" Fabric A squares to top corners of unit from step 1 as shown. Press. Make fifty-six.

A = 2 x 2

Make 56

LEAF BORDER CORNERS

1. Draw a diagonal line on wrong side of 7" light Fabric E square. Place one light and one dark 7" Fabric E square right sides together. Sew a scant 1/4" away from drawn line on both sides to make half-square triangles as shown. Make two. Cut on drawn line and press. This will make four half-square triangles. Square to 6 1/2".

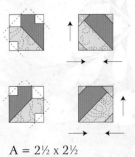

E = 7 x 7
E = 7 x 7
Make 2

Square to 6 1/2
Make 4

2. Making quick corner triangle units, sew two 2" Fabric A squares and one 2 1/2" Fabric A square to unit from step 1 as shown. Press. Make four, two of each variation.

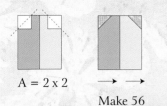

A = 2 1/2 x 2 1/2
2 x 2
Make 4
(2 of each variation)

3. Sew 1 1/2" x 6 1/2" Fabric A strip to unit from step 2 as shown. Press. Make four, two of each variation.

6 1/2   1 1/2

1 1/2

6 1/2

Make 2   Make 2

4. Sew 1 1/2" x 7 1/2" Fabric A strip to unit from step 3 as shown. Press. Make four, two of each variation.

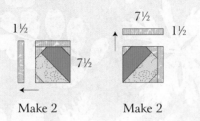

1 1/2

7 1/2

7 1/2   1 1/2

Make 2   Make 2

5. Sew 1 1/2" x 7 1/2" Accent Border piece to unit from step 4 as shown. Press. Make four, two of each variation.

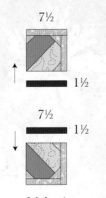

7 1/2

1 1/2

7 1/2

1 1/2

Make 4
(2 of each variation)

ADDING THE BORDERS

1. Sew 1 1/2" x 42" Accent Border strips together end to end to make one continuous 1 1/2"-wide strip. Cut two 1 1/2" x 60 1/2" and two 1 1/2" x 96 1/2" Accent Border strips. Sew 1 1/2" x 60 1/2" strips to top and bottom of quilt. Press seams toward border.

2. Referring to quilt layout on page 83 and photo on page 81, arrange and sew twelve Border Leaf units into a row. Press seams to one side. Make two. Rows measure 6 1/2" x 60 1/2". Arrange and sew sixteen Border Leaf units into a row. Press seams to one side. Make two. Rows measure 6 1/2" x 80 1/2".

3. Sew eight 1 1/2" x 42" Fabric A strips together end to end to make one continuous 1 1/2"-wide strip. Cut two 1 1/2" x 60 1/2" and two 1 1/2" x 80 1/2" strips. Referring to quilt layout on page 83, sew 1 1/2"-wide strips to matching size Border Leaf rows. Press toward Fabric A. Sew shorter Border Leaf rows to top and bottom of quilt. Press toward Accent Border.

4. Sew two 1 1/2" x 96 1/2" Accent Border strips from step 1 to sides of quilt. Press seams toward Accent borders.

5. Referring to quilt layout on page 83 and photo on page 81, arrange and sew a Corner Leaf Unit to each end of remaining Border Leaf rows. Press. Make two.

6. Sew Border Leaf rows from step 5 to sides of quilt. Press seams toward Accent border.

LAYERING AND FINISHING

1. Cut backing crosswise into three equal pieces. Sew pieces together to make one 85" x 120" (approximate) backing piece. Press. Arrange and baste backing, batting, and top together, referring to Layering the Quilt on page 110.

2. Hand or machine quilt as desired.

3. Sew the 2 3/4" x 42" binding strips end to end to make one continuous 2 3/4"-wide strip. Refer to Binding the Quilt on page 111 and bind quilt to finish.

GARDEN GLORIES QUILT
October
DAHLIA
BLOCK OF THE MONTH

October Block of the Month Dahlia (Left Center) Garden Glories Quilt photo page 10		
FIRST CUT		
	Number of Strips or Pieces	Dimensions
Fabric A Background 1/3 yard	1	10 1/2" square
Fabric B Flower Petals 1/4 yard		
Fabric C Flower Pistil 1/8 yard		
Flower Center Scraps	1	4 1/2" circle
	2	4" circles

Cutting

Refer to templates on the following page. From Fabric B cut eight full flower petals and eight top section petals. From Fabric C cut eight flower pistils. Refer to Making Yo-Yo's and Circle Templates on page 107 to cut flower center circles.

Assembly

1. With right sides together, sew top section to flower petal across curved end as shown using a 1/4" seam allowance. Clip, turn, and press petal. Make eight.

Make 8

2. With right sides together, fold flower pistil in half lengthwise. Sew across top angled edge as shown. Clip corner, turn right side out as shown, and press seam edge only. Make eight.

Seam

Fold

Fold

3. Place flower pistil on petal, aligning raw edges. Place another petal piece on top, right sides together. Sew these pieces together with a 1/4"-wide seam allowance. Open petals spreading and centering pistil over seam just sewn. Press seam open. Make four.

Hint: A small craft stick can aid in spreading and smoothing pistil.

Make 4

4. Sew two petal units from step 3 and one pistil from step 2 together. Press. Make two. Sew halves together, inserting remaining pistil units between petals. Press.

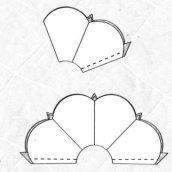

5. Pin or baste dahlia to center of 10½" Fabric A square. Fold back two pistils to stitch along seam line, ½" from curved petal edges, and back down other seam line as shown. Repeat for each petal or appliqué dahlia to block.

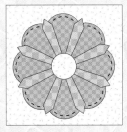

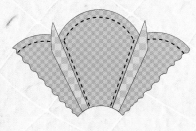

Block measures
10½" square

6. Refer to page 107 for 4" Circle Template. For large flower center, place two 4" circles right sides together and stitch around edge with a ¼"-wide seam allowance. Clip curve and slit center of back circle; turn right side out. Press. Pin at center of appliquéd dahlia and top stitch ¼" from edge of circle.

7. For small flower center use the 4½" Circle Template on page 107. Make Flower Center Yo-Yo following the directions on page 107. After quilting is completed, sew yo-yo to center of block.

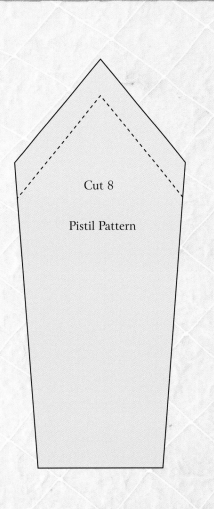

Cut 8

Pistil Pattern

Garden Glories Quilt - Dahlia Block
Flower Petal Patterns

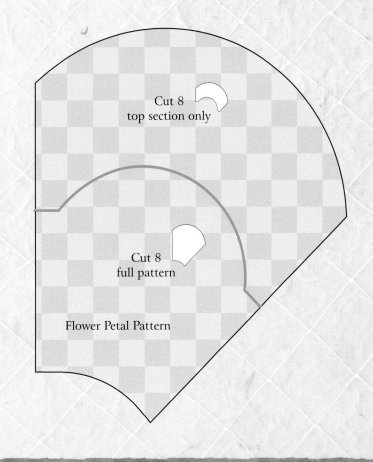

Cut 8
top section only

Cut 8
full pattern

Flower Petal Pattern

Not quite ripe!

November 3
The garden is pretty
much put to bed for the
winter. A few last bulbs
need to be planted before
the ground freezes hard.
We're still harvesting a
few carrots and squash.

We'll have some fresh garden produce to enjoy at Thanksgiving.
Many reasons to be thankful!

Fresh crunchy
carrots

Colorful Leaf

Autumn Welcome Basket

I don't think I'll ever
finish raking the leaves ... although it's pleasant
work ... fresh crisp air, the sound dried leaves make when you
step on them, the colorful piles ready for the compost bin ...
Life is good.

Checklist
☐ Finish planting bulbs
☑ Harvest and store
 remaining vegetables
☑ Turn and water compost
☐ Transplant hardy
 perennials

Ripe Squash

COLOR PENCIL
COLOR PENCIL

AUTUMN'S BOUNTY

36" ROUND TABLE TOPPER

Rejoice in nature's bounty with this colorful table topper, perfect for your Thanksgiving table. Felted wool provides rich color and texture to this easy sewing project. Use on the table or mount on the wall for an unusual autumn accent.

FABRIC REQUIREMENTS AND CUTTING INSTRUCTIONS

Read all instructions before beginning and use 1/4" -wide seam allowances throughout. Read Cutting the Strips and Pieces on page 108 prior to cutting fabrics.

Autumn's Bounty Table Topper		
36" Round	FIRST CUT	
	Number of Strips or Pieces	Dimensions
■ Background 2¹/8 yards wool or felt	2	36" circles
Fruit and Leaves 1/6 - 1/4 yard (of each color) assorted felts and wools –Allow for shrinkage		Assorted greens, golds, oranges, reds, purples, yellows, and browns
#8 Perle Cotton Fabric Stabilizer - 2 yards		

TIPS FOR APPLIQUÉING WITH WOOL

Use felt or felted wool for this design. There is no need to add seam allowances or to turn under edges for felted wool. We used unwashed felt for the Background and backing, but felted all other pieces. To felt your own wool, follow these steps:

1. Plunge the wool fabric in boiling water for 5 minutes, then plunge it into icy water until very chilled. Do not mix colors as dyes may run.

2. Blot the wool with a dry towel and place both towel and wool in the dryer until thoroughly dry. The result is a thicker, fuller fabric that will give added texture to the table topper. Pressing felted wool is not recommended as it will flatten the texture. Remember, most wools will shrink up to 10% when boiled.

APPLIQUÉING THE TABLE TOPPER

1. Trace appliqué patterns on pages 91-92 for pineapple and its decorative shapes, orange, apple, lemon, plum, grapes, walnut, and leaves.

2. Use assorted scraps to cut two pineapples and their decorative shapes, two pineapple leaves, two oranges, twenty-two large and eight small grapes, two apples, four lemons, eight lemon leaves, four walnuts, eight grape leaves, and twenty-six oak leaves.

3. Use temporary spray adhesive or pins to attach stabilizer to wrong side of 36" felt circle. Refer to quilt layout and photo on page 89. Position appliqués on background circle. Pin, baste, or glue in place prior to stitching. Use hand or machine blanket stitch to attach the appliqués to the background circle in order of positioning. Use matching thread.

ASSEMBLY

1. Remove stabilizer if desired. Pin second background circle to wrong side of appliquéd circle.

2. Refer to Embroidery Stitch Guide on page 108. Use number 8 perle cotton and a blanket stitch to sew edges of circles together with matching thread.

Tip

To make a 36" diameter circle pattern we used yardstick compass points (available at quilt and craft shops) placed 18" apart on a yardstick to draw a 36" circle on paper.

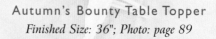

Autumn's Bounty Table Topper
Finished Size: 36"; Photo: page 89

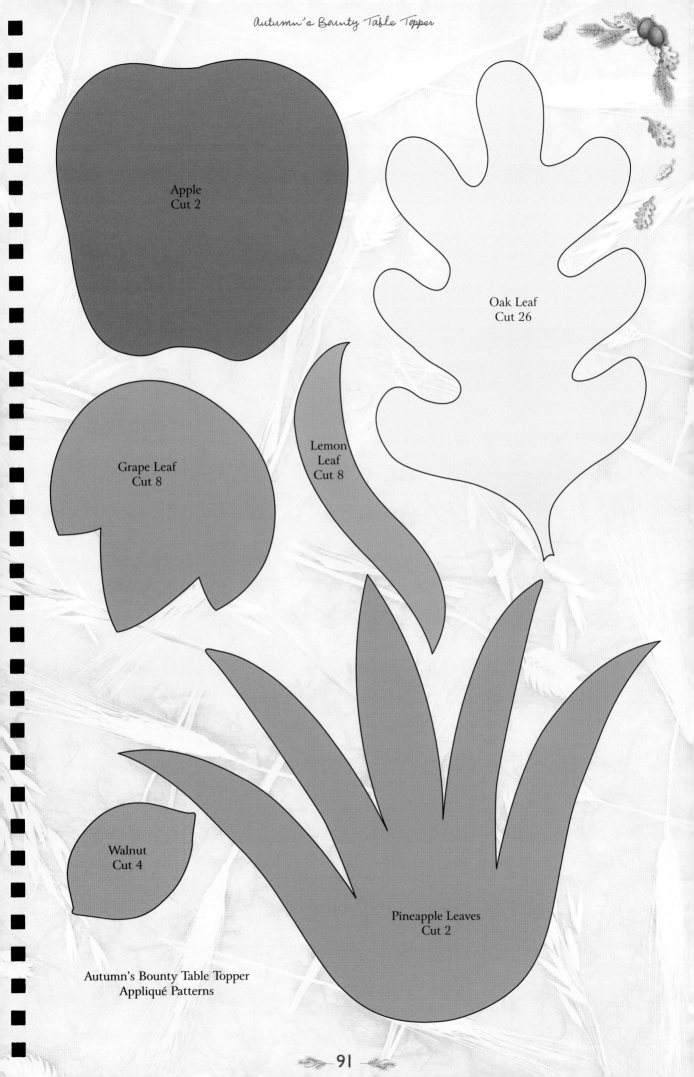

Apple
Cut 2

Oak Leaf
Cut 26

Grape Leaf
Cut 8

Lemon
Leaf
Cut 8

Walnut
Cut 4

Pineapple Leaves
Cut 2

Autumn's Bounty Table Topper
Appliqué Patterns

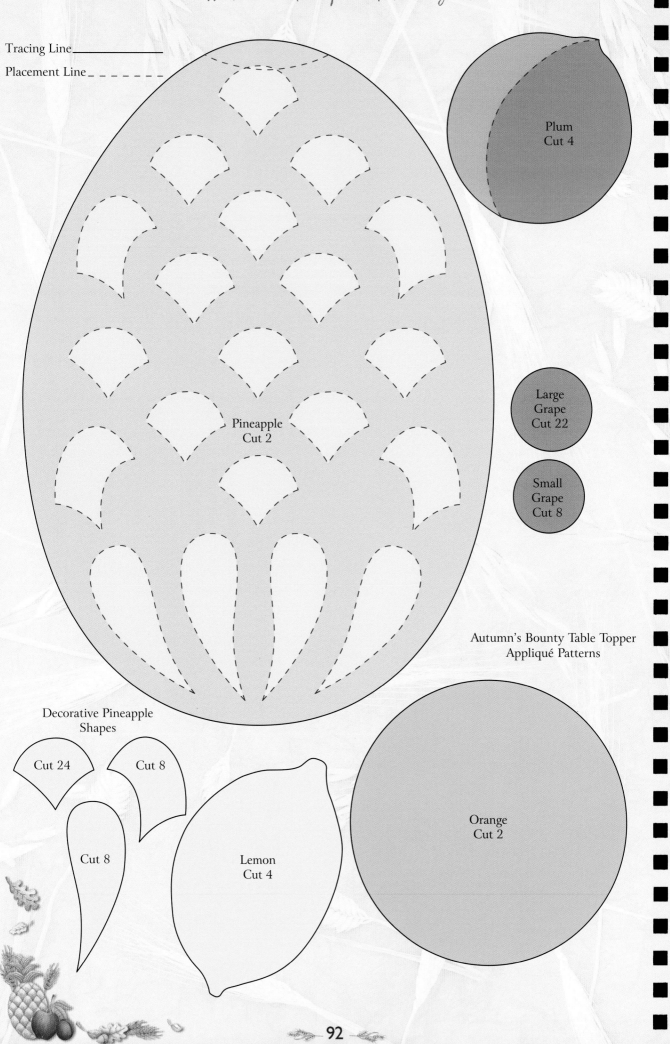

Tracing Line _____
Placement Line _ _ _ _

Plum
Cut 4

Pineapple
Cut 2

Large
Grape
Cut 22

Small
Grape
Cut 8

Autumn's Bounty Table Topper
Appliqué Patterns

Decorative Pineapple
Shapes

Cut 24

Cut 8

Cut 8

Orange
Cut 2

Lemon
Cut 4

Fall Frames

Juicy Plum

Enjoy the colors and textures of autumn all through the year with this unique accessory. These leaves look fresh off the tree when displayed on a twig background. We used a twig placemat for our textural background, but the same look can be achieved using twigs cut to length and glued on a cardboard backing. Hanging on a wall or placed on a shelf, this fabulous frame is the perfect home accent.

Materials Needed:

Simple unfinished wooden frame
 with deep rabbet edge
Twig placemat or twigs glued to
 cardboard
Pressed leaves (see page 49)
Handmade paper (available at art
 supply or scrapbook store)
Wood sealer
Acrylic paints: dark green and black
Antiquing medium
Assorted brushes
Matte spray varnish
E6000® Glue

Preparing the Frame

Remove glass and seal unfinished wooden frame with wood sealer. When dry, sand lightly, remove sanding residue, and paint frame with dark green paint. When paint is dry, sand edges to "distress" the frame. Apply antiquing medium following manufacturer's directions. When the frame is dry, mix water with black paint and fill an old toothbrush with watered down paint. Rub your thumb over the bristles to add black paint spatters to the frame. Practice this technique on a piece of paper before trying it on the frame. When frame is completely dry, spray with several coats of matte spray varnish, following manufacturer's directions.

Preparing the Leaves

Cut twigs (or placemat) to fit inside the frame and glue to cardboard. Size of handmade paper rectangles will depend on leaf size. For greater interest, paper should be slightly smaller than the leaves so that leaves extend past the paper rectangle. Tear paper to the size desired using the following method: draw a rectangle in the desired size on the back side of the paper. Using a paintbrush, wet the paper on the drawn line, allowing the paper to absorb the water. Place a towel along drawn line then place a ruler on top of the towel. Lifting toward you, use the ruler as a straight edge, and "tear" the paper along drawn line. Repeat for all sides. This procedure will give you soft edges on all sides of the paper.

Determine placement of the leaves on the paper backgrounds and glue leaves to the paper rectangles. When dry, determine placement of the paper/leaves on the twig background and glue in place.

Clean glass and place leaf picture inside frame, backing with more cardboard if desired. Add picture hanger or display on a plate rack as shown.

GARDEN GLORIES QUILT
November
EMPEROR'S CROWN
BLOCK OF THE MONTH

November Block of the Month Emperor's Crown (Top Right) Garden Glories Quilt photo page 10		
FIRST CUT		
	Number of Strips or Pieces	Dimensions
Fabric A Background *1/3 yard*	1	6 1/2" square
	6	2 1/2" squares
	1	1 1/2" x 9 1/2"
	1	1 1/2" x 8 1/2"
	2	1 1/2" x 4 1/2"
	3	1 1/2" x 2 1/2"
	19	1 1/2" squares
Fabric B Dark Flower Petal *Scrap*	2	1 1/2" x 3 1/2"
	4	1 1/2" squares
Fabric C Medium Flower Petal *1/8 yard*	3	2 1/2" squares
	1	1 1/2" x 3 1/2"
	1	1 1/2" square
Fabric D Light Flower Petal *1/8 yard*	3	2 1/2" squares
	1	1 1/2" x 3 1/2"
	1	1 1/2" square
Fabric E Dark Leaf *Scrap*	1	2 1/2" square
	2	1 1/2" x 2 1/2"
Fabric F Light Leaf *1/8 yard*	3	1 1/2" x 4 1/2"
	1	1 1/2" x 3 1/2"
	2	1 1/2" x 2 1/2"
	2	1 1/2" squares

Assembly

1. Referring to Quick Corner Triangles on page 108, sew 2 1/2" Fabric A square to 2 1/2" Fabric C square as shown. Press. Make two. Repeat process using 2 1/2" squares to make two Fabric A/D combinations and one Fabric C/D combination. Press.

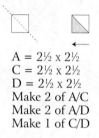

A = 2½ x 2½
C = 2½ x 2½
D = 2½ x 2½
Make 2 of A/C
Make 2 of A/D
Make 1 of C/D

2. Sew 1 1/2" Fabric A square to 1 1/2" Fabric F square. Press. Make two. Sew to 1 1/2" x 2 1/2" Fabric A piece as shown. Press. Make two.

1½   1½
☐ 1½   ☐ ▨ 2½
▨ 1½
Make 2   Make 2

3. Sew one A/C unit from step 1 to unit from step 2 as shown. Press. Sew one A/D unit from step 1 to remaining unit from step 2. Press.

4. Making quick corner triangle units, sew two 1 1/2" Fabric A squares to 1 1/2" x 3 1/2" Fabric B piece as shown. Press. Make two.

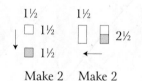

A = 1½ x 1½
B = 1½ x 3½
Make 2

5. Making quick corner triangle units, sew 1 1/2" Fabric A square to 1 1/2" x 3 1/2" Fabric D piece and 1 1/2" Fabric A square to 1 1/2" x 3 1/2" Fabric C piece as shown. Press.

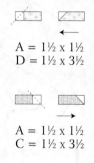

A = 1½ x 1½
D = 1½ x 3½

A = 1½ x 1½
C = 1½ x 3½

6. Sew units from step 5 to units from step 4 as shown. Press.

7. Making quick corner triangle units, sew 1 1/2" Fabric D square to 1 1/2" x 2 1/2" Fabric E piece, and 1 1/2" Fabric C square to 1 1/2" x 2 1/2" Fabric E piece as shown. Press.

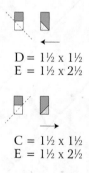

D = 1½ x 1½
E = 1½ x 2½

C = 1½ x 1½
E = 1½ x 2½

8. Sew units from step 6 to units from step 7 as shown. Press.

9. Sew units from step 3 to units from step 8 as shown. Press.

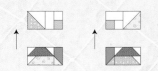

10. Making quick corner triangle units, sew two 1 1/2" Fabric A squares to opposite corners of 2 1/2" Fabric E square as shown. Press.

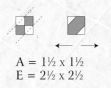

A = 1½ x 1½
E = 2½ x 2½

11. Sew unit from step 10 and three remaining units from step 1 together as shown. Press.

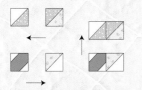

12. Making quick corner triangle units, sew 1 1/2" Fabric A square to 1 1/2" x 2 1/2" Fabric F piece as shown. Press. Make two, one of each variation.

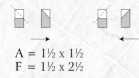

A = 1½ x 1½
F = 1½ x 2½

13. Making quick corner triangle unit, sew 1 1/2" Fabric A square to 1 1/2" Fabric B square as shown. Press. Make 2. Sew unit to 1 1/2" Fabric A square as shown. Press. Make one of each variation.

A = 1½ x 1½
B = 1½ x 1½
Make 2

1½   1½

☐ ◼ 1½   ◪ ☐ 1½
  ←   →

Make one of each variation

14. Sew units from step 12 to units from step 13 as shown. Press. Make two, one of each variation.

15. Sew units from step 14 to 2 1/2" Fabric A squares as shown. Press. Sew units together. Press.

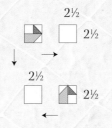

16. Sew units from steps 9, 11, and 15 together as shown. Press. Block measures 8 1/2" square.

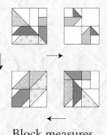

Block measures 8½" square

17. Making quick corner triangle unit, sew 1 1/2" Fabric A square to 1 1/2" Fabric B square. Press. Make two.

☐ ◤
  →

A = 1½ x 1½
B = 1½ x 1½
Make 2

18. Sew 1 1/2" x 4 1/2" Fabric F piece between one unit from step 17 and 1 1/2" Fabric A square as shown. Press. Sew 1 1/2" x 4 1/2" Fabric F piece between remaining unit from step 17 and 1 1/2" x 2 1/2" Fabric A piece as shown. Press.

19. Sew 1 1/2" x 4 1/2" Fabric A piece to 1 1/2" x 3 1/2" Fabric F piece. Press. Sew 1 1/2" x 4 1/2" Fabric A piece to 1 1/2" x 4 1/2" Fabric F piece. Press.

20. Sew units from step 18 to sides of 6 1/2" Fabric A square as shown. Press. Sew to units from step 19 as shown. Press. Sew to 1 1/2" x 8 1/2" and 1 1/2" x 9 1/2" Fabric A pieces. Press. Block measures 9 1/2" square.

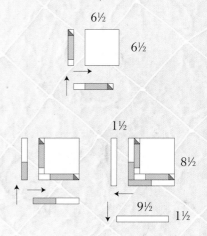

21. Draw a diagonal line on the unit as shown. Stitch 1/8" from each side of the drawn line. Carefully cut the unit on the drawn line to make two leaf units. Sew a leaf unit to two sides of the Emperor's Crown Block as shown. Press.

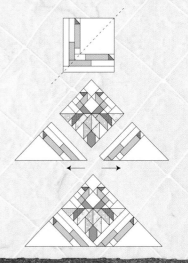

filbert

Winter Garden~
Beauty of bare twigs
Red touches of winter berries
Delicate shape of shrubs
Texture of bark
~ Time for all to rest

Cotoneaster

English Ivy

Holiday Evergreen

Brazil nut

December 8

Snow frosts my evergreens, creating a magical winter landscape in my garden. A heap of snow mounds on the birdbath, making it look like a giant snow cone. Pine boughs fill the house with the savory scents of Christmas. I mixed red roses with evergreens for the centerpiece on the dining room table. What a beautiful combination with the tan tablecloth!

Mountian Ash

Yew   *Yew berry*

My favorites to cut for decorating~
~ Oregon Grape-gorgeous scalloped leaves
~ Silvery blue juniper
~ Bird's Nest Spruce
~ Cotoneaster-nice red berries
~ Mugho Pine-great filler

Balsam fir

Touch of green

Snow-dusted pinecones

CHRISTMAS ROSE

55" SQUARE LAP QUILT

The charm and beauty of roses in winter is portrayed in this warm and inviting lap quilt. A variety of appliqué techniques makes the intricate rose design easier than it looks. The vine is cut and quick-fused in a single piece to make this stunning effect easy to accomplish.

FABRIC REQUIREMENTS AND CUTTING INSTRUCTIONS

Read all instructions before beginning and use 1/4"-wide seam allowances throughout. Read Cutting the Strips and Pieces on page 108 prior to cutting fabrics.

Christmas Rose Lap Quilt 55" x 55"		
	FIRST CUT	
	Number of Strips or Pieces	Dimensions
Fabric A Background Squares 5/8 yard each of two fabrics	2 for each fabric	17 1/2" squares
Fabric B Flowers & Buds 1/4 yard each of four fabrics		
Fabric C Star Center & Accent Flowers 1/8 yard each of four fabrics		
Fabric D Leaves & Stems 1/6 yard each of four fabrics		
Fabric F Vine 1/2 yard	4	3" x 40 1/2"

Christmas Rose Lap Quilt Continued		
	FIRST CUT	
	Number of Strips or Pieces	Dimensions
BORDERS		
Fabric G Border Triangles and Outside Border 1 3/8 yards	4	6 1/2" squares
	5	3 1/2" x 42"
	56	3 1/2" squares
Fabric H Border Triangles 5/8 yard	28	3 1/2" x 6 1/2"
First Border 1/4 yard	4	1 1/2" x 42"
Second Border 1/2 yard	4	3 1/2" x 42"
Third Border 1/4 yard	5	1 1/2" x 42"
Binding 1/2 yard	6	2 3/4" x 42"
Backing - 3 1/2 yards Batting - 61" x 61" Lightweight fusible web - 1 1/4 yards (may vary depending on method used)		

MAKING THE QUILT

You will be making four Christmas Rose Appliqué Blocks, an appliquéd border, and a pieced border. Refer to Accurate Seam Allowance on page 108 prior to sewing pieced border. Whenever possible, use the Assembly Line Method on page 108. Press in direction of arrows. Block measures 16 1/2" unfinished.

CHRISTMAS ROSE BLOCKS

The patterns given are for the quick-fuse appliqué method. To hand appliqué, add 1/4" seam allowances when cutting appliqué pieces.

1. Refer to Hand Appliqué or Quick-Fuse Appliqué directions on page 109 for your preferred method of appliqué. Trace Christmas Rose Templates from page 103 onto an 8 1/2" x 11" paper, matching dashed lines as indicated to complete pieces. Photocopy the traced templates four times and tape the four pattern sections together to make a completed appliqué block pattern.

2. From your pattern, trace section A-2 for center rose. Trace section B-1 for center star shape. For each block, cut one A-2 joined, one B-1 joined, four C-1 and four C-1 reversed, five A-1, and four of each remaining piece.

3. Fold 17 1/2" Fabric A square in half vertically and horizontally to mark center and quarter sections. Trace completed appliqué block pattern onto background square.

4. Referring to block layout below, position and stitch appliqués on background square. Make four blocks, alternating the position of each red fabric from block to block. Square completed blocks to 16½".

Block measures 16½" square

ASSEMBLY

1. Refer to quilt layout and photo on page 97. Arrange and sew blocks in two horizontal rows of two blocks each. Press seams in opposite directions in each row.

2. Sew rows together. Press.

3. Cut two 1½" x 32½" First Border strips. Sew to top and bottom of quilt. Press toward border.

4. Cut two 1½" x 34½" First Border strips. Sew to sides of quilt. Press toward border.

5. Cut two 3½" x 34½" Second Border strips. Sew to top and bottom of quilt. Press toward border.

6. Cut two 3½" x 40½" Second Border strips. Sew to sides of quilt. Press toward border.

7. Sew the 1½" x 42" Third Border strips end to end to make one continuous 1½"-wide strip. Cut two 1½" x 40½" Third Border strips. Sew to top and bottom of quilt. Press toward border.

8. Cut two 1½" x 42½" Third Border strips. Sew to sides of quilt. Press toward border.

Christmas Rose Lap Quilt
Finished Size: 55" x 55"; Photo: page 97

APPLIQUÉING THE SECOND BORDER

1. You will be making a mitered frame from which your vine will be cut. Draw a 45° diagonal line on the wrong side of each corner of four 3" x 40½" Fabric F strips. Place strips in pairs, right sides together, and stitch ¼" from drawn line on one end of each pair to form a seam as shown. Place sewn pairs, right sides together, and sew remaining corners at a 45° angle. Finger press seams open.

40½   45° angle

3

2. Place sewn square frame on top of Second Border to check fit. Fabric frame should be an exact match of Second Border. Adjust if necessary. Trim seams to ¼"-wide and press seam allowances open.

3. Refer to quilt layout on page 99 and photo on page 97 to determine number and placement of vine curves. Refer to Quick-Fuse Appliqué directions on page 109. Make templates for vine and A-1 circle pattern on page 102. Cut forty-eight A-1 circles.

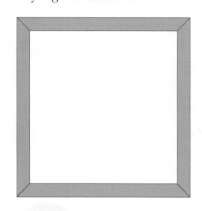

4. Cut fusible web into four 3" x 42" strips. Referring to quilt layout on page 99 and photo on page 97, trace vine pattern onto fusible web. Cut ¼" beyond traced lines. Fuse to wrong side of vine fabric frame. Cut along traced lines.

5. Position and fuse vine and circles to Second Border. Referring to Machine Appliqué directions on page 109, blanket-stitch vine to Second Border or use other decorative stitching as desired.

Entries

------- ------- ------- ------- ------- ------- -------

------- ------- ------- ------- ------- ------- -------

------- ------- ------- ------- ------- ------- -------

------- ------- ------- ------- ------- ------- -------

------- ------- ------- ------- ------- ------- -------

------- ------- ------- ------- ------- ------- -------

------- ------- ------- ------- ------- ------- -------

------- ------- ------- ------- ------- ------- -------

------- ------- ------- ------- ------- ------- -------

ADDING THE OUTSIDE BORDER

1. Refer to Quick Corner Triangles and Accurate Seam Allowance on page 108. Sew two 3½" Fabric G squares to a 3½" x 6½" Fabric H piece as shown. Press. Make twenty-eight.

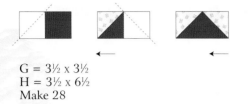

G = 3½ x 3½
H = 3½ x 6½
Make 28

2. Sew together seven units from step 1 as shown. Press seam allowances to one side. Make four. Unit measures 3½" x 42½".

Make 4 rows

3. Sew 3½" x 42" Fabric G strips end to end to make one continuous 3½"-wide strip. Cut strip into four 3½" x 42½" strips. Sew unit from step 2 to 3½" x 42½" Fabric G piece as shown. Press. Make four.

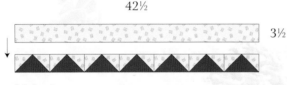

42½

3½

Make 4

4. Sew one unit from step 3 between two 6½" Fabric G squares. Press. Make two.

6½   6½

6½

Make 2

5. Refer to quilt layout on page 99. Sew units from step 3 to top and bottom of quilt. Press.

6. Sew units from step 4 to sides of quilt. Press.

LAYERING AND BINDING

1. Cut backing in half crosswise. Sew pieces together. Press. Cut backing to 61" square. Arrange and baste backing, batting, and top together, referring to Layering the Quilt on page 110.

2. Hand or machine quilt as desired.

3. Sew 2¾" x 42" binding strips end to end to make one 2¾"-wide binding strip. Refer to Binding the Quilt on page 111 and bind quilt to finish.

Juniper Sprig with Snow

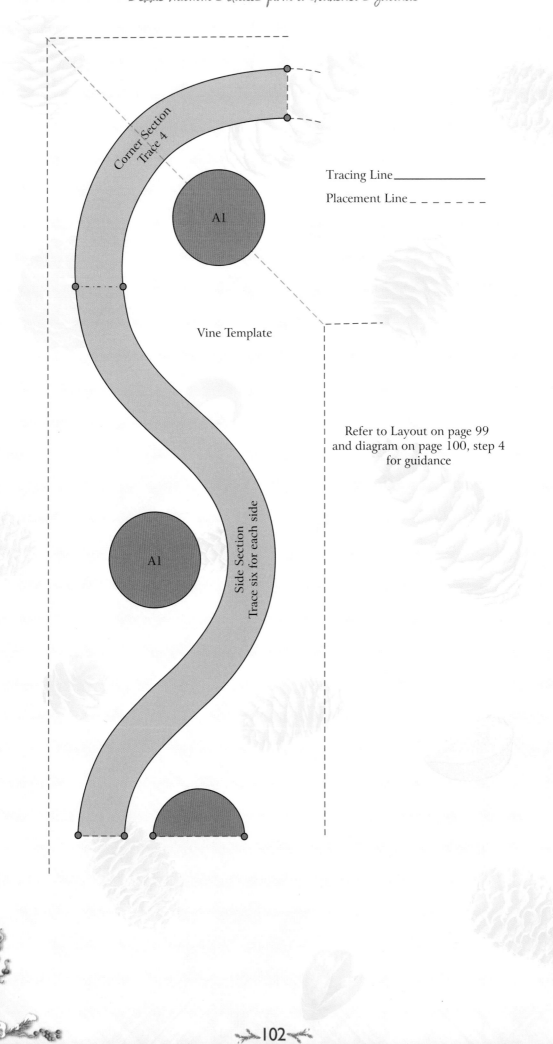

Corner Section
Trace 4

A1

Tracing Line _____
Placement Line _ _ _ _ _ _ _

Vine Template

Refer to Layout on page 99
and diagram on page 100, step 4
for guidance

A1

Side Section
Trace six for each side

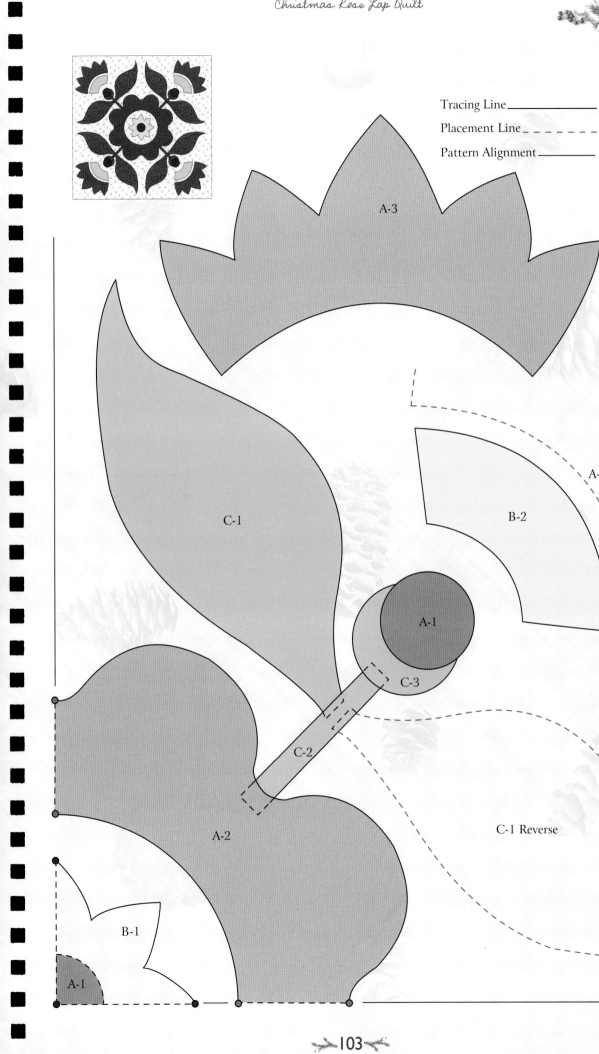

Tracing Line———————

Placement Line— — — — —

Pattern Alignment———————

A-3

A-3 Placement Line

C-1

B-2

A-1

C-3

C-2

A-2

C-1 Reverse

B-1

A-1

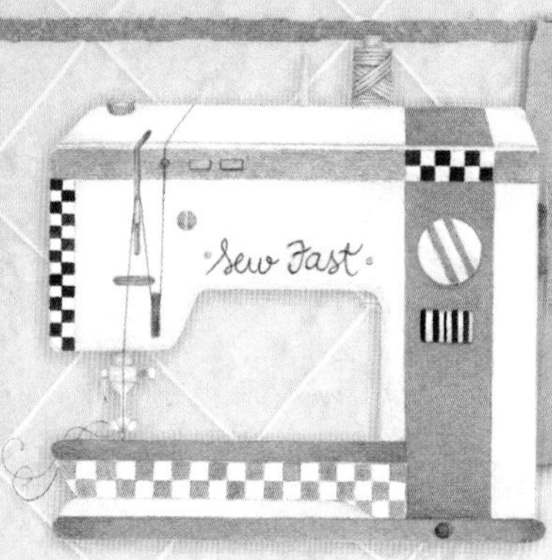
Sew Fast

GARDEN GLORIES QUILT

December QUILT ASSEMBLY

BLOCK OF THE MONTH

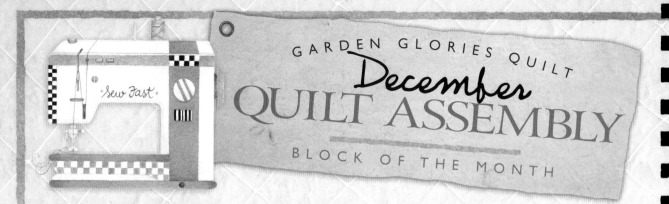

Fabric Requirements and Cutting Instructions

Read all instructions before beginning and use 1/4"-wide seam allowances throughout. Read Cutting the Strips and Pieces on page 108 prior to cutting fabrics.

Garden Glories Quilt photo page 10

December Block of the Month Finishing the Quilt 67" x 67"	FIRST CUT		SECOND CUT	
	Number of Strips or Pieces	Dimensions	Number of Pieces	Dimensions
FLORAL ACCENT BLOCK				
Floral Center Panel *1 yard**	2	6" x 42"	4	6" x 17 3/4"
**if repeating stripe fabric is used for Outside Border, enough fabric remains for these cuts*				
Panel Accent *1/2 yard*	2 4	2 1/2" x 42" 2 1/4" x 42"	 8	 2 1/4" x 17 3/4"
BORDERS				
Sashing *5/8 yard*	12	1 1/2" x 42"	4	1 1/2" x 25 3/4"
Center/First Border *1/3 yard*	4	2 1/2" x 42"		
Second Border *1/4 yard*	4	1 1/2" x 42"		
Outside Border *3 2/3 yards (directional)*	8	4 1/2" x 43"		
Binding *5/8 yard*	7	2 1/2" x 42"		
Backing - 4 1/8 yards Batting - 74" x 74"				

Making Center Panel

1. Sew 6" x 17 3/4" Floral Center Panel between two 2 1/4" x 17 3/4" Panel Accent strips. Press. Make four.

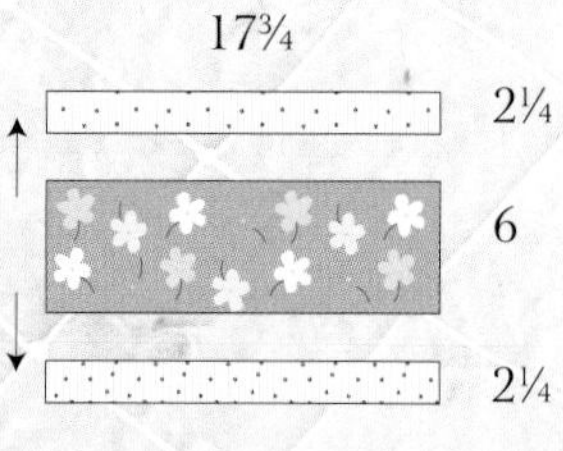
17¾
2¼
6
2¼

Make 4

2. Sew 2 1/2" x 42" Panel Accent strips between two 1 1/2" x 42" Sashing strips. Press. Make two strip sets. Cut strip sets into eight 4 1/2" x 9 1/2" segments.

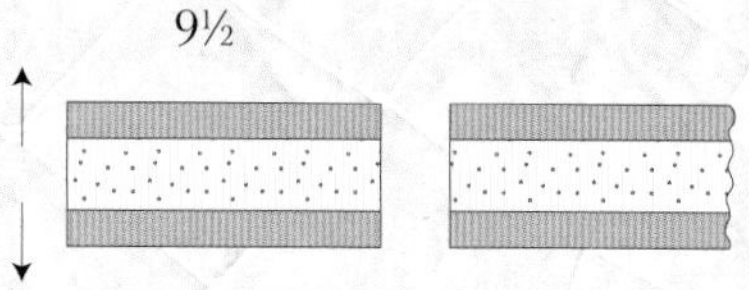
9½

Make 2 strip sets
Cut 8

3. Sew Floral Center Panel unit from step 1 between two segments from step 2. Press. Make four units. Press. Sew each unit to 1 1/2" x 25 3/4" Sashing strip as shown. Press. Make four.

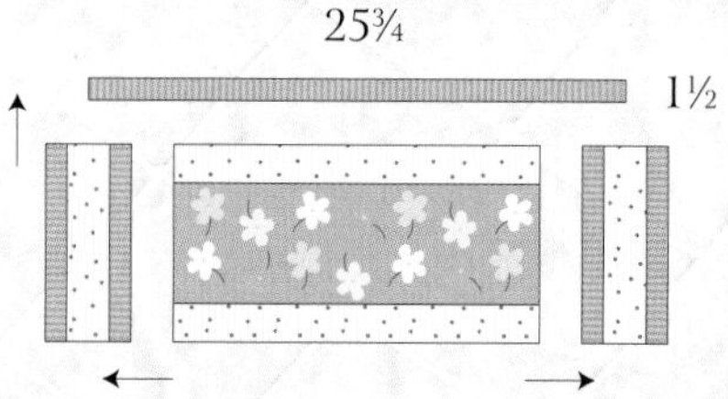
25¾
1½

Make 4

4. Referring to quilt layout, sew Birdbath Center Panel between two units from step 3. Refer to quilt layout and photo on page 10 to arrange flower blocks. Sew unit from step 3 between two 10 1/2" flower blocks. Press. Make two. Sew units to Birdbath Center Panel. Press. Center unit measures 45 3/4" square.

Adding Corner Blocks

1. Sew 2½" × 42" Center/First Border strip between 1½" × 42" Sashing and 1½" × 42" Second Border strips as shown. Press. Make four strip sets. Cut each strip set in half crosswise to make a total of eight segments.

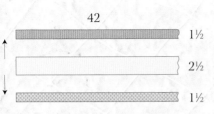

42

1½

2½

1½

Make 4 strip sets
Cut into 8 segments

2. Sew one strip segment to pieced Fritillary Block as shown. Press. Sew appliquéd July Bug Cornerstone to end of one strip segment as shown. Press. Sew to pieced corner block. Press. Repeat with remaining three Bug blocks and three flower units to complete four corner blocks.

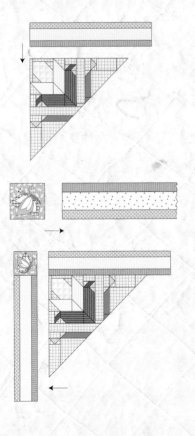

3. Referring to Mitered Borders on page 110, sew two 4½" × 43" Outside Border strips to pieced corner blocks from step 2 as shown, mitering corners. Press. Make four. Mark each Outside Border 33" from corner as shown. Align ruler along bottom of triangle from marked point to point. Draw a line across borders and trim on drawn line.

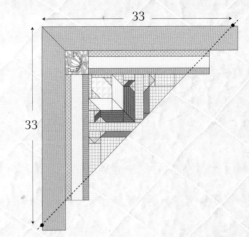

33

33

4. Referring to quilt layout and photo on page 10, sew unit from step 3 to each side of center panel. Press.

Garden Glories Block of the Month Quilt
Finished Size: 67" x 67"; Photo: page 10

Layering and Finishing

1. Cut backing crosswise into two equal pieces. Sew the pieces together to make one 74" x 84" (approximate) backing piece. Cut backing to 74" x 74". Arrange and baste backing, batting, and quilt top together referring to Layering the Quilt directions on page 110.

2. Hand or machine quilt as desired.

3. Sew 2¾" x 42" Binding strips end to end to make one continuous 2¾"-wide strip. Refer to Binding the Quilt directions on page 111 and bind quilt to finish.

Embellishments

Refer to quilt photo on page 10 and layout on page 105 to position flower centers, yo-yos, and buttons. Use three strands of embroidery floss and a stem stitch to embroider stamens for Day Lily. Sew three beads at tips.

Making Ruched Flowers

1. Place 2"-wide Fabric D strip right side down; fold raw edges of strip lengthwise to meet at center. Press. Fold in half lengthwise and press. Strip should measure ½"-wide. With pencil, mark bottom edge at 1" intervals. Mark top edge at 1" intervals starting ½" from end.

double fold

single fold

2. Beginning at the top, hand-baste through all layers from top mark to bottom mark and back to the next top mark forming a zigzag pattern. Make stitches approximately ⅛" long. Gently pull thread tight, gathering fabric to approximately one-third of original size, forming a row of petal-like shapes. Knot end.

3. To make flower, coil three of the petal shapes to form the center. Secure in place. Continue coiling around until the flower is approximately 3"-wide, securing and tucking under raw ends. After quilting is complete, stitch ruched flower to quilt. Sew button to center of flower.

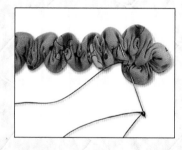

Making Yo-Yos

1. Trace desired Yo-Yo Template on wrong side of fabric and cut out on drawn line.

2. Hold the circle with the wrong side facing you. Fold edge toward you turning 1/4" and use quilting thread to sew short running stitches close to folded edge.

Wrong side

3. Pull thread tightly to gather into a smaller circle. Make several invisible "tacking" stitches to secure the thread.

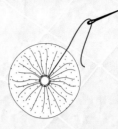

4. Refer to color photo and quilt layout to position and tack yo-yos in place.

Yo-Yo and Circle
Templates

1½"
1¾"
2"
2¼"
2½"

3"

3½"

4"

4½"

5"

5½"

Embroidery Floss

General Directions

CUTTING THE STRIPS AND PIECES

Before you make each of the projects in this book, pre-wash and press the fabrics. Using a rotary cutter, see-through ruler, and a cutting mat, cut the strips and pieces for the project. If indicated on the Cutting Chart, some will need to be cut again into smaller strips and pieces. Make second cuts in order shown to maximize use of fabric. The approximate width of the fabric is 42". Measurements for all pieces include $1/4$"-wide seam allowance unless otherwise indicated. Press in the direction of the arrows.

ASSEMBLY LINE METHOD

Whenever possible, use the assembly line method. Position pieces right sides together and line up next to sewing machine. Stitch first unit together, then continue sewing others without breaking threads. When all units are sewn, clip threads to separate. Press in direction of arrows.

ACCURATE SEAM ALLOWANCE

Accurate seam allowances are always important, but especially when the quilt top contains multiple pieced borders with lots of blocks and seams! If each seam is off as little as $1/16$", you'll soon find yourself struggling with components that just won't fit. To ensure you are stitching a perfect $1/4$"-wide seam, try this simple test.

Cut three strips of fabric, each exactly $1 1/2$" x 12". With right sides together, and long raw edges aligned, sew two strips together, carefully maintaining a $1/4$" seam. Press. Add the third strip to complete the strip set. Press seams to one side and measure. The finished strip set should measure $3 1/2$" x 12". The center strip should measure 1"-wide, the two outside strips $1 1/4$"-wide, and the seam allowances exactly $1/4$". If your measurements differ, check to make sure that you have pressed the seams flat. If your strip set still doesn't "measure up," try stitching a new strip set, adjusting the seam allowance until you are able to achieve a perfect $1/4$"-wide seam.

EMBROIDERY STITCH GUIDE

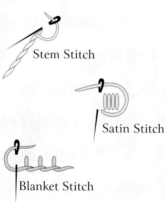

Stem Stitch

Satin Stitch

Blanket Stitch

French Knot

QUICK CORNER TRIANGLES

Quick corner triangles are formed by simply sewing fabric squares to other squares or rectangles. The directions and diagrams with each project illustrate what size pieces to use and where to place squares on the corresponding piece. Follow steps 1–3 below to make corner triangle units.

1. With pencil and ruler, draw diagonal line on wrong side of fabric square that will form the triangle. See Diagram A. This will be your sewing line.

A.
sewing line

2. With right sides together, place square on corresponding piece. Matching raw edges, pin in place and sew ON drawn line. Trim off excess fabric, leaving $1/4$" seam allowance as shown in Diagram B.

B.
trim $1/4$" away from sewing line

3. Press seam in direction of arrow as shown in step-by-step project diagram. Measure completed corner triangle unit to ensure the greatest accuracy.

C.
finished corner triangle unit

Partridge Berries

QUICK-FUSE APPLIQUÉ

Quick-fuse appliqué is a method of adhering appliqué pieces to a background with fusible web. For quick and easy results, simply quick-fuse appliqué pieces in place. Use sewable, lightweight fusible web for the projects in this book unless indicated otherwise. Finishing raw edges with stitching is desirable. Laundering is not recommended unless edges are finished.

1. With paper side up, lay fusible web over appliqué design. Leaving $1/2$" space between pieces, trace all elements of design. Cut around traced pieces, approximately $1/4$" outside traced line. See Diagram A.

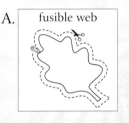

A. fusible web

2. With paper side up, position and iron fusible web to wrong side of selected fabrics. Follow manufacturer's directions for iron temperature and fusing time. Cut out each piece on traced line. See Diagram B.

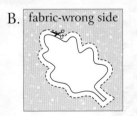

B. fabric-wrong side

3. Remove paper backing from pieces. A thin film will remain on wrong side of fabric. Position and fuse all pieces of one appliqué design at a time onto background, referring to color photos for placement. Fused design will be the reverse of traced pattern.

APPLIQUÉ PRESSING SHEET

An appliqué pressing sheet is very helpful when there are many small elements to apply using a quick-fuse appliqué technique. The pressing sheet allows small items to be bonded together before applying them to the background. The sheet is coated with a special material that prevents the fusible web from adhering permanently to the sheet. Follow manufacturer's directions. Remember to let the fabric cool completely before lifting it from the appliqué sheet. If not cooled, the fusible web could remain on the sheet instead of the fabric.

MACHINE APPLIQUÉ

This technique should be used when you are planning to launder quick-fuse projects. Several different stitches can be used: small narrow zigzag stitch, satin stitch, blanket stitch, or another decorative machine stitch. Use an appliqué foot if your machine has one. Use a stabilizer to obtain even stitches and help prevent puckering. Always practice first to check your machine settings.

1. Fuse all pieces following Quick-Fuse Appliqué directions.

2. Cut a piece of stabilizer large enough to extend beyond the area you are stitching. Pin to the wrong side of fabric.

3. Select thread to match appliqué.

4. Following the order that appliqués were positioned, stitch along the edges of each section. Anchor beginning and ending stitches by tying off or stitching in place two or three times.

5. Complete all stitching, then remove stabilizers.

HAND APPLIQUÉ

Hand appliqué is easy when you start out with the right supplies. Cotton or machine embroidery thread is easy to work with. Pick a color that matches the appliqué fabric as closely as possible. Use appliqué or silk pins for holding shapes in place and a long, thin needle, such as a sharp, for stitching.

1. Make a template for every shape in the appliqué design. Use a dotted line to show where pieces overlap.

2. Place template on right side of appliqué fabric. Trace around template.

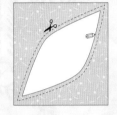

3. Cut out shapes $1/4$" beyond traced line.

4. Position shapes on background fabric, referring to quilt layout. Pin shapes in place.

5. When layering and stitching appliqué shapes, always work from background to foreground. Where shapes overlap, do not turn under and stitch edges of bottom pieces. Turn and stitch the edges of the piece on top.

6. Use the traced line as your turn-under guide. Entering from the wrong side of the appliqué shape, bring the needle up on the traced line. Using the tip of the needle, turn under the fabric along the traced line. Using blind stitch, stitch along the folded edge to join the appliqué shape to the background fabric. Turn under and stitch about $1/4$" at a time.

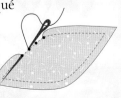

ADDING THE BORDERS

1. Measure quilt through the center from side to side. Trim two border strips to this measurement. Sew to top and bottom of quilt. Press toward border.

2. Measure quilt through the center from top to bottom, including borders added in step 1. Trim border strips to this measurement. Sew to sides and press. Repeat to add additional borders.

MITERED BORDERS

1. Cut the border strips or strip sets as indicated for quilt.

2. Measure each side of the quilt and mark center with a pin. Fold each border unit crosswise to find its midpoint and mark with a pin. Using the side measurements, measure out from the midpoint and place a pin to show where the edges of the quilt will be.

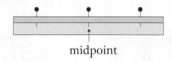

midpoint

3. Align a border unit to quilt. Pin at midpoints and pin-marked ends first, then along entire side, easing to fit if necessary.

4. Sew border to quilt, stopping and starting 1/4" from pinmarked end points. Repeat to sew all four border units to quilt.

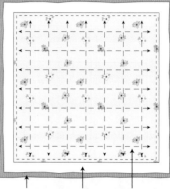

quilt front

5. Fold corner of quilt diagonally, right sides together, matching seams and borders. Place a long ruler along fold line extending across border. Draw a diagonal line across border from fold to edge of border. This is the stitching line. Starting at 1/4" mark, stitch on drawn line. Check for squareness, then trim excess. Press seam open.

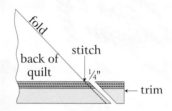

LAYERING THE QUILT

1. Cut backing and batting 4" to 8" larger than quilt top.

2. Lay pressed backing on bottom (right side down), batting in middle, and pressed quilt top (right side up) on top. Make sure everything is centered and that backing and batting are flat. Backing and batting will extend beyond quilt top.

backing   batting   quilt top

3. Begin basting in center and work toward outside edges. Baste vertically and horizontally, forming a 3"– 4" grid. Baste or pin completely around edge of quilt top. Quilt as desired. Remove basting.

Holly Branch

BINDING MITERED CORNERS
GREATER THAN 90° ANGLE

1. Place a pin 1/4" from point of angle as shown. This will be the stopping point for the miter.

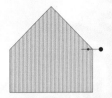

2. Sew binding on edge of quilt, having raw edges even with quilt edge. Stop stitching at pin. Remove quilt and clip threads.

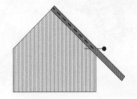

3. Pull binding strip to extend off edge of quilt; keeping a straight line with quilt edge. This makes a little tuck in the binding at pin point.

4. Lay binding strip down over tucked area even with edge of quilt, and continue stitching.

5. Press binding away from quilt. Fold binding to back, adjusting corners as needed to complete miters on back of quilt. Pin miters as needed. Hand stitch in place.

90° ANGLE CORNERS

1. Place a pin 1/4" away from corner. Sew binding on edge of quilt, stopping at pin. Remove quilt and clip threads. Continue in same manner as described at left to make miter and finish binding.

BINDING THE QUILT

1. Trim batting and backing to 1/4" beyond raw edge of quilt top. This will add fullness to binding.

2. Fold and press binding strips in half lengthwise with wrong sides together.

3. Lay binding strips on top and bottom edges of quilt top with raw edges of binding and quilt top aligned. Sew through all layers, 1/4" from quilt edge. Press binding away from quilt top. Trim excess length of binding.

4. Sew remaining two binding strips to quilt sides through all layers including binding just added. Press and trim excess length.

5. Folding top and bottom first, fold binding around to back then repeat with sides. Press and pin in position. Hand stitch binding in place.

← fold top and bottom binding in first

FINISHING PILLOWS

1. Layer batting between pillow top and lining. Baste. Hand or machine quilt as desired, unless otherwise indicated. Trim batting and lining even with raw edge of pillow top.

2. Narrow hem one long edge of each backing piece by folding under 1/4" to wrong side. Press. Fold under 1/4" again to wrong side. Press. Stitch along folded edge.

3. With right sides up, lay one backing piece over second piece so hemmed edges overlap, making single backing panel the same measurement as the pillow top. Baste backing pieces together at top and bottom where they overlap.

Baste

Baste

4. With right sides together, position and pin pillow top to backing. Using 1/4"-wide seam, sew around edges, trim corners, turn right side out, and press.

PILLOW FORMS

Cut two Pillow Form fabrics to finished size of pillow plus 1/2". Place right sides together, aligning raw edges. Using 1/4"-wide seam, sew around all edges, leaving 4" opening for turning. Trim corners and turn right side out. Stuff to desired fullness with polyester fiberfill and hand-stitch opening closed.

Discover More from Debbie Mumm®

Here's a sampling of the many quilting and home décor books by Debbie Mumm®. These books are available at your local quilt shop, by calling (888) 819-2923, or by shopping online at www.debbiemumm.com.

Quilting Through The Year with Debbie Mumm®
80-page, soft cover

Debbie Mumm's® Floral Inspirations
80-page, soft cover

Debbie Mumm's® Country Settings
112-page, soft cover

Debbie Mumm® Celebrates The Holidays at Home
80-page, soft cover

Debbie Mumm® Quilts Santa's Scrapbook
112-page, soft cover

Debbie Mumm's® 12 Days of Christmas
140-page, soft cover

Debbie Mumm® Salutes America the Beautiful
32-page, soft cover

Debbie Mumm's® Sweet Baby Dreams
24-page, soft cover

Friendship Quilt Collection
36-page, soft cover

Book titles limited to stock on hand. Products may be discontinued at any time by Debbie Mumm, Inc.

Debbie Mumm, Inc.
1116 E. Westview Court,
Spokane, WA 99218

Toll Free (888) 819-2923
(509) 466-3572
Fax (509) 466-6919

www.debbiemumm.com

Credits

DESIGNS BY DEBBIE MUMM®

Special thanks to my creative teams:

EDITORIAL & PROJECT DESIGN

Carolyn Ogden: Managing Editor
Georgie Gerl: Quilt and Craft Designer
Carolyn Lowe: Quilt and Craft Designer
Laura M. Reinstatler: Technical Editor/Writer
Jane Townswick: Writer/Editor
Maggie Bullock: Copy Editor
Jackie Saling: Craft Designer
Nancy Kirkland: Seamstress/Quilter
Wanda Jeffries: Machine Quilter
Pam Clarke: Machine Quilter
Sandy Schreven: Seamstress
Bonnie Swannack: Seamstress

BOOK DESIGN & PRODUCTION

Mya Brooks: Production Director
Tom Harlow: Graphics Manager
Sherry Hassel: Sr. Graphic Designer
Heather Hughes: Graphic Designer
Nancy Hanlon: Graphic Designer
Robert H. Fitzner: Graphic Designer

PHOTOGRAPHY

Peter Hassel Photography
Debbie Mumm® Graphics Studio

ART TEAM

Lou McKee: Senior Artist/Designer
Kathy Arbuckle: Artist/Designer
Sandy Ayars: Artist
Heather Butler: Artist
Kathy Eisenbarth: Artist
Gil-Jin Foster: Artist

Special thanks to Lou McKee and David VerWolf for allowing us to use their garden for on-location photography. Thanks also to Gina and Paul Sundberg for providing the garden gate setting for our photography. We also want to thank Mike and Charleen Swisher at Prairie House Lavender for providing the setting for our Lavender Fields Bed Quilt photography. October scrapbook background Copyright Design by Glad Tidings.

©2003 Debbie Mumm, Inc.
Printed in Hong Kong